Never a Worm This Long

Donna Alvermann
Connie A. Bridge
Barbara A. Schmidt
Lyndon W. Searfoss
Peter Winograd

 D.C. Heath and Company
HEATH Lexington, Massachusetts   Toronto, Ontario

Acknowledgments

Grateful acknowledgment is made for permission to reprint the following copyrighted material.

Barrett, Judi. **Cloudy With a Chance of Meatballs** is reprinted by permission of Macmillan Publishing Company. Text copyright © 1978 by Judi Barrett. Drawings copyright © 1978 by Ron Barrett.

Blume, Judy. "**Friends for Life**," by Judy Blume, reprinted by permission of G.P. Putnam's Sons from *Once Upon a Time,* copyright © 1986 by G.P. Putnam's Sons.

Blume, Judy. **The Pain and the Great One,** copyright © 1974 by Judy Blume, reprinted by permission of Macmillan Publishing Company.

Broekel, Ray, and Laurence White, Jr. **Hocus Pocus: Magic You Can Do,** copyright © 1984 by Ray Broekel and Laurence White, Jr. Reprinted by permission of Albert Whitman and Company.

Bulla, Clyde Robert. From **A Grain of Wheat: A Writer Begins**; copyright © 1985; reprinted by permission of David R. Godine, Publishers, Inc.

Ciardi, John. "**Why Pigs Cannot Write Poems**," from *Doodle Soup,* by John Ciardi. Copyright © 1985 by Myra J. Ciardi. Reprinted by permission of Houghton Mifflin Company.

Clapp, Patricia. "**The Magic Book Shelf**"; copyright © 1972 by Patricia Clapp; reprinted from *Plays,* The Drama Magazine for Young People, by permission of Plays, Inc., 120 Boylston Street, Boston, MA 00116. This play is for reading purposes only; for permission to produce, write to the publisher.

Cleary, Beverly. "**Ramona Reads**," adaptation of *Ramona Quimby, Age 8,* by Beverly Cleary. Copyright © 1981 by Beverly Cleary. Adapted by permission of William Morrow & Company, Inc.

DeRoin, Nancy. "**Good Deeds**," from *Jataka Tales,* edited by Nancy DeRoin. Copyright © 1975 by Nancy DeRoin. Reprinted by permission of Houghton Mifflin Company.

Greaves, Margaret. **Once There Were No Pandas (A Chinese Legend),** copyright © 1985 by Margaret Greaves. Reprinted by permission of Dutton Children's Books and Methuen Children's Books, Ltd.

Harelson, Randy. "**Pick a Pen Pal**," from *Swak: The Complete Book of Mail Fun for Kids.* Copyright © 1985. Reprinted by permission of Workman Publishing Co., Inc.

Harkness, Ruth. "**I Find Su-lin**," from *The Lady and the Panda.* Copyright 1938 by Carrick & Evans, Inc. Copyright renewed 1966 by Mrs. Nelson Anderson. Mrs. Warren R. Burdick, and Mrs. James McCombs. Reprinted by permission of J.B. Lippincott Company.

Hitte, Kathryn, and William D. Hayes. "**Mexicali Soup**," adapted from *Mexicali Soup.* Copyright © 1970 Parents Magazine Press, a division of Gruner & Jahr USA Publishing.

Hurwitz, Johanna. Adaptations of Chapters 1 and 7 in **The Adventures of Ali Baba Bernstein,** by Johanna Hurwitz. Copyright © 1985 by Johanna Hurwitz. Reprinted by permission of William Morrow & Company, Inc.

Lamorisse, Albert. **The Red Balloon,** by Albert Lamorisse. Copyright © 1956 by Albert Lamorisse. Reprinted by permission of Doubleday & Company, Inc.

Livingston, Myra Cohn. "**My Other Name**," from *A Song I Sang to You,* by Myra Cohn Livingston. Copyright © 1958, 1959, 1965, 1967, 1969, and 1984 by Myra Cohn Livingston. Reprinted by permission of Marian Reiner.

Mosel, Arlene. **Tikki Tikki Tembo,** retold by Arlene Mosel, illustrated by Blair Lent. Copyright © 1968 by Arlene Mosel. Adapted by permission of Henry Holt and Company, Inc.

Munro, Helen S. **Dear Aunt Helen,** copyright © 1985 by Helen S. Munro. Reprinted by permission of the Author.

Peck, Robert Newton. "**Quarter for a Haircut**," from *Soup and Me.* Copyright © 1975 by Robert Newton Peck; reprinted by permission of Random House, Inc.

Pitt, Valerie. **Let's Find Out About Names.** Copyright © 1971 by Valerie Pitt; reprinted by permission of Franklin Watts, Inc.

Prelutsky, Jack. "**I Met a Dragon Face to Face**" is reprinted by permission of G.P. Putnam's Sons from *Once Upon A Time,* copyright © 1986 by G.P. Putnam's Sons.

Rockwell, Thomas. From **How to Eat Fried Worms**; copyright © 1973 by Thomas Rockwell; reprinted by permission of the publisher Franklin Watts, Inc.

(Continued on page 368)

Table of Contents

Pandas

That's Write!

Abracadabra!

You Name It!

D.E.A.R. Drop Everything And Read

A Good Deed, Indeed!

Never a Worm This Long

Incredible Edibles

How many edible things can you find?

Bocca-Wacca-Wattamus

They took Ryan O'Brien to breakfast
   and asked what he wanted to eat.
His mother looked very nervous
   as he wiggled around in his seat.

"I want bocca-wacca-wattamus and salamander stew,
Riggle-raggle ragamuffins, rutabagas, too.
I want diffy-daffy dandelions and then, for my dessert,
a dish of loony lingaberries smothered with fresh dirt."

"Ryan!" squealed his mother.
"Wow!" said his sister.
"Yuck!" said his brother.
"We're all out," said the waiter.

They took Ryan O'Brien to lunch
    at the best restaurant in the town.
His mother looked very nervous
    as the family began to sit down.

"I want bocca-wacca-wattamus and salamander stew,
Riggle-raggle ragamuffins, rutabagas, too.
I want diffy-daffy dandelions and then, for my dessert,
a dish of loony lingaberries smothered with fresh dirt."

        "Ryan!" squealed his mother.
            "Wow!" said his sister.
            "Yuck!" said his brother.
    "Not in season," said the waitress.

They took Ryan O'Brien to dinner
    "And what will you have today?"
His mother looked very nervous
    as Ryan began to say:

"I want bocca-wacca-wattamus and salamander stew,
Riggle-raggle ragamuffins, rutabagas, too.
I want diffy-daffy dandelions and then, for my dessert,
a dish of loony lingaberries smothered with fresh dirt."

        "Ryan!" squealed his mother.
            "Wow!" said his sister.
            "Yuck!" said his brother.
        "Medium or rare?" said the waiter.

—Barbara Schmidt

How to Eat Fried Worms

adapted from the book by Thomas Rockwell

PART ONE

The Bet

Alan and Billy came up the front walk. Tom was sitting on his porch steps, bouncing a tennis ball.

"Hey, Tom! Where were you last night?"

"My mother kept me in."

"What for?" asked Alan.

"I wouldn't eat my dinner."

"What was it?" said Billy.

"Salmon."

"Wouldn't she let you just eat two bites?" asked Alan. "Sometimes my mother says, well, all right, if I'll just eat two bites."

"I wouldn't eat even one," answered Tom.

"That's stupid," said Billy. "I'd eat one bite of anything before I'd get sent to my room."

Tom shrugged.

"How about mud?" Alan asked Billy. "You wouldn't eat a bite of mud."

"Sure, I would," Billy said. "Mud. What's mud? Just dirt with a little water in it."

"How about worms?" Alan asked Billy. "You wouldn't eat a bite of worms."

"Sure I would," said Billy. "Why not? Worms are just dirt."

"Yeah, but they bleed."

"So you'd have to cook them."

"I bet a hundred dollars you wouldn't really eat a worm. You talk big now, but you wouldn't if you were sitting at the dinner table with a worm on your plate."

"I bet I would. I'd eat *fifteen* worms if somebody bet me a hundred dollars."

"You really want to bet? *I'll* bet you fifty dollars you can't eat fifteen worms. I really will."

"Where are you going to get fifty dollars?"

"In my savings account. I've got one hundred and thirty dollars."

"Your mother wouldn't let you take it out."

"She would if I lost the bet. She'd have to. I earned the money mowing lawns, so I can do whatever I want with it. I'll bet you fifty dollars you can't eat fifteen worms. Come on. You're chicken. You know you can't do it."

Billy was hesitating as Joe came scuffing up the walk. "What's going on?" asked Joe.

"Come on," said Alan to Billy. "Tom can be your second and Joe will be mine, just like a duel. You think it's so easy—"

"Okay," said Billy, "but regular worms. They can't be caterpillars or those green worms that get on tomatoes."

"And he can eat them any way he wants," said Tom. "Boiled, stewed, or fried."

"Okay, but we choose the worms," said Joe. "And there have to be witnesses present when he eats them. Not just you and Billy."

"Okay?" Alan said to Billy.

Billy scratched his ears. How bad could a worm taste? He'd eaten fried liver, salmon loaf, mushrooms, tongue, pig's feet. If he won fifty dollars, he could buy that bike George Cunningham's brother had promised to sell him in September when he went away to college. He could gag *anything* down for fifty dollars, couldn't he?

He looked up. "I can use ketchup or mustard or anything like that? As much as I want?"

Alan nodded. "Okay?"

Billy stood up. "Okay."

The First Worm

Alan and Tom and Joe leaned on their shovels under a tree in the apple orchard. They were watching the worms they had dug squirming on a flat rock.

"Not him," said Tom, pointing to a night crawler.

"Why not?"

"Look at it. It would choke a dog."

"It's this one or nothing," said Alan, picking up the night crawler.

Tom thought about it. It *would* be more fun watching Billy trying to eat the night crawler. He grinned. Boy it was *huge!* Wait till Billy saw it.

"All right. Come on." He turned and started back toward the house, dragging his shovel.

As he waited in the barn, Billy set out bottles of ketchup and mustard, a box of crackers, salt and pepper shakers, a lemon, and some horseradish.

It wasn't long before Tom's head appeared around the door.

"Ready?"

Billy scrambled up, brushing back his hair. "Yeah."

"TA DAHHHHHHHHH!" Tom flung the door open; Alan marched in carrying a covered platter. Joe was slouching along beside him with a napkin over one arm, nodding and smiling. Alan swept the cover off the platter.

"*Awrgh!*" cried Billy.

The huge night crawler sprawled in the center of the platter, brown and steaming.

"Boiled," said Tom. "We boiled it."

Billy stormed about the barn. "A night crawler isn't a *worm!* If it was a worm, it'd be called a worm. A night crawler is a night crawler."

Joe ran off to get his father's dictionary:

> *night crawler n:* EARTHWORM; esp: a large
> earthworm found on the top of the soil at
> night.

Billy kicked a barrel. It still wasn't fair. He didn't care what any dictionary said. Everybody knew the difference between a night crawler and a worm.

Yugh! He poked it with his finger.

Alan said they agreed at the start that he and Joe could choose the worms. If Billy was going to cheat, the bet was off. He said he had other things to do besides argue all day with a fink.

Tom took Billy aside and talked to him about George Cunningham's brother's bike. Sure, it was a big worm but it was only a couple of bites. Did he want to lose a bike over *two bites?*

"I could probably eat this one. But I got to eat *fifteen.*"

Tom sat Billy down and tied the napkin around his neck. Then he handed him the fork.

Billy gazed at the dripping ketchup and mustard, thinking, *Awrgh!* It's all right talking about eating worms, but *doing* it!

"Glug." Billy poked the fork into his mouth, chewed furiously, *gulped!* . . . gulped! . . .

"How did it taste?" asked Alan.

"Good, good," said Billy. "Very fine, very fine."

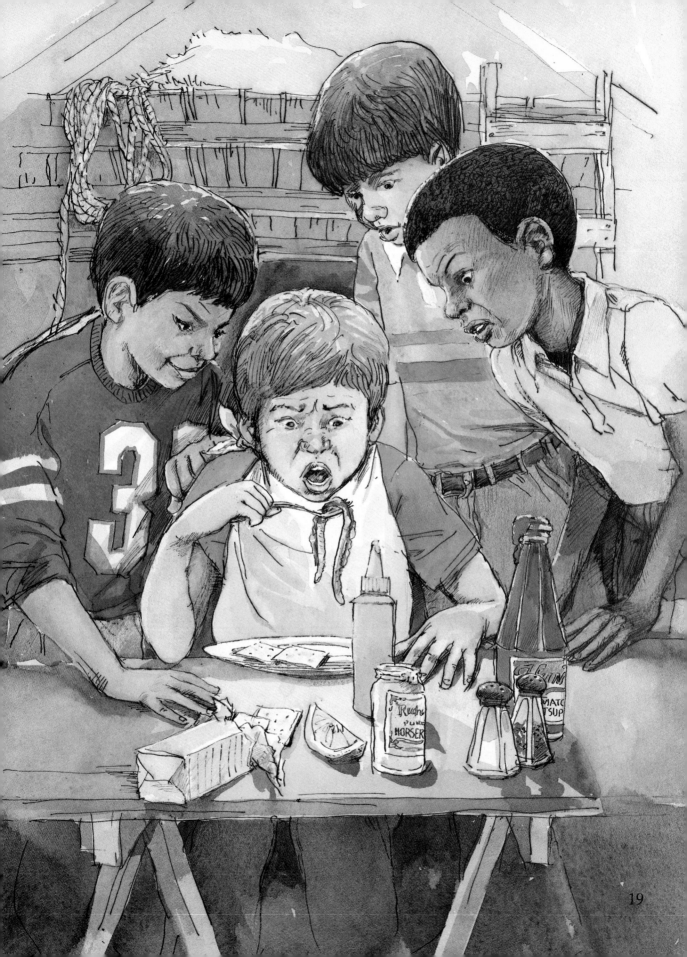

Alan and Joe don't want to lose the bet, so they plan to make the rest of the worms more difficult to eat.

The Plan

Alan and Joe stopped in the orchard.

"You think he'll be able to do it?" asked Alan, biting his nails.

"I don't know," said Joe.

"He can't do it," said Alan. "How could anybody eat fifteen worms?"

"Forget it," said Joe. "If he doesn't give up himself, I'll figure something out. We could spike the next worm with pepper. He'd eat one piece and then another. Then all of a sudden he'd sneeze: ka-chum! Then he'd sneeze again: ka-*chum!* Then again: ka-chum ka-chum! He'll clutch his stomach. His eyes will begin to water. Ka-chum! Ka-chum!"

"Billy's awful stubborn," said Alan. "Even if it was killing him, he might not give up. Remember last summer? It was 95 degrees in the shade and I dared him to put on all his winter clothes and his father's coat and his snow boots and walk up and down Main Street all afternoon."

"Yeah, I remember," said Joe. "If he doesn't quit, then we'll think of something different. We'll think up new ways of getting him to stop with every worm."

PART TWO

Alan and Joe have been scheming to keep Billy from winning the bet. They tried to scare him into not eating worms by telling him that he would get a strange disease. They also tried sending him a fake note from a doctor saying it wasn't healthy to eat worms. So far, Billy has eaten eight worms. Alan and Joe are worried about losing. Here's what they think of next.

The Ninth Worm

"That's not a worm!" yelled Billy. "How can it be a worm? Geez, it must be two feet long!"

"It's a worm," said Alan stubbornly. "It's just like all the others. I rolled it in cornmeal and fried it."

"It's over two feet long!" screeched Billy.

He knew something was up. Otherwise Joe wouldn't be pretending to be gazing up at the clouds. Billy noticed he kept glancing at Alan and him. Something was up.

"Look," said Alan. "I'll cut it. You can see for yourself it's a worm. There. See? Come on. Eat up. We haven't got all day."

Billy poked at the huge worm with his fork. Something sure was up. He ate the piece Alan had cut. He looked the rest of the worm over carefully as he chewed. He ate another bite. *Arrgh!* He'd forgotten to dip it in the horseradish sauce.

"Come on, come on, come on," said Alan.

"Yeah," said Joe. "Eat up, Billy. We got to go."

I'll never be able to eat the whole thing, thought Billy. "It'd choke me, it's too much yuck at once. There's never been a worm this long."

"Okay," said Alan. "Then the bet's off. Come on, Joe. He chickened out. Let's go."

"All right, all right," said Billy, playing for time. "The whole thing."

"You'll make yourself sick," said Alan.

He's too anxious, thought Billy. What's going on? He ate another bite. Then he began to scrape the cornmeal carefully off the worm with his knife.

"What are you doing?" said Alan.

"I think I'll have it plain today. No cornmeal."

"That's not fair! You can't—"

"Glue!" screamed Billy all of a sudden. "Glue! You glued two crawlers together! Gee! Tom! Tom, look what they tried to pull! Glue!"

Panting, Tom bent over the plate. "You're right. Geez!"

"That's cheating!" said Billy. "I ought to win right now. You cheated."

"Fifteen worms in fifteen days!" yelled Joe. "You haven't won yet!"

"But you *cheated!*" shouted Tom.

"It wasn't cheating," Joe yelled at Billy. "It didn't *work!* You didn't *fall for it!* If you'd eaten the whole thing and *then* found out it was two worms glued together, *then* you could have claimed to win because Alan was cheating. If you'd eaten it, it would have been cheating. But you didn't, so it's not. The bet's still on."

Alan and Joe are concerned that Billy really will eat the fifteen worms. Though they've tried, they decide they can't scare him out of eating worms. They try keeping Billy so busy that he will forget to eat a worm a day. So far, with Tom's help, Billy has been too clever. Billy has eaten most of the fifteenth worm and is about to win the bet when Joe and Alan grab him. They get into a fight. Billy's father hears the boys fighting. He goes to break it up and sends Billy to his room. It seems like the bet is over . . .

Who Wins?

Billy kicked the bed. He'd *won*. All he'd had to do was eat two more bites, two *bites*. What had his father gotten so mad for? *Alan* was the one who started the fight.

Now he was going to lose? He was stuck in his room! After all he'd gone through? All for nothing?

Billy kicked the wall. *Two bites*. What difference could *two bites* have made?

Tom's younger brother Pete suddenly appeared below the window.

"THE WORM! BILLY!" Pete had brought him a worm. The fifteenth worm!

Billy opened the window.

"Catch!" yelled Pete.

"Hurry!"

Alan and Joe came running into the yard.
They were waving their arms and shouting at the
top of their lungs.

"TOO LATE!" yelled Billy.

Throwing back his head, he dropped the
squirming night crawler into his mouth . . .
chewed and chewed.

"Too late! I win," gasped Billy. "I *win*."

After the Win

Billy leaned his new bike against a tree. Tom and Joe and Alan were already sitting by the river, opening their lunch bags.

"What have you got for lunch?" asked Tom.

Billy looked embarrassed.

"Worm-and-egg on rye."

"Why can't you ever bring something somebody else likes, so you can trade?"

Billy frowned. He opened his lunch bag.

"I don't know. I just can't stop. I don't dare tell my mother. I even like the *taste* now." He scratched his head. "Do you think I could be the first person who's ever been *hooked* on worms?"

Think About It

1. What's unusual about the eating habits of Ryan O'Brien and Billy?
2. How do the families of both boys react to their weird eating habits?
3. What was surprising about the ending of the poem? Of the story?
4. How would you solve the problem of stopping Ryan from ordering strange-sounding foods? Of getting Billy unhooked on fried worms?

Create and Share   Invite Billy to your own home-cooked worm dinner. Write a note telling him the time, date, address, and menu. Describe how you will serve the worms. Tell what other foods you will serve with the worms. Draw a picture of your dinner.

Explore   Bring a real or made-up menu to class. Explain how you would use your menu to order your favorite meal.

MEXICALI SOUP

adapted from a story
by Kathryn Hitte and William D. Hayes

Characters

MAMÁ	RICARDO	ADELA
TERESA	TOMÁS	PAPÁ
	RUBÉN	

Setting: A city in the southwestern part of the United States.

MAMÁ: *(walking down a street, talking to herself)* Only the best of everything! Potatoes and peppers—the best! Tomatoes and beans— the best! The best garlic and corn! And then, cooked all together, ah! Mamá's special Mexicali Soup. The soup that always makes everyone say, "Mamá makes the best soup in the world." Ah, dinner tonight will be very special for my Adela and Ricardo and Tomás and Rubén and Teresa, and for Papá too.

TERESA: *(runs out of school with a friend)* Mamá, Mamá! Wait a minute. May I play awhile with Ann? Please?

MAMÁ: Very well. Awhile. But don't be late for dinner. I'm making my special soup tonight.

TERESA: Mmm-mmm, Mexicali Soup! *(looks thoughtful)* But, Mamá?

MAMÁ: Yes, Teresa?

TERESA: Mamá, there are such a lot of potatoes in your Mexicali Soup.

MAMÁ: *(smiles)* Of course.

TERESA: Ann doesn't eat potatoes. Her mother doesn't eat them. Her sister doesn't eat them. Potatoes make you fat, Mamá. I think we should do what others do here. We're no longer in our town in Mexico, Mamá, where everyone eats potatoes. We're in the city now. So would you, Mamá, would you please leave out the potatoes?

MAMÁ: No potatoes? *(looks carefully at Teresa)* Well, there are plenty of good things in the Mexicali Soup without the potatoes. I'll put in more of everything else. It will still make good soup.

TERESA: Of course it will. You make the best soup in the world. *(runs off with Ann)*

MAMÁ: *(turns onto a street with little stores still talking to herself)* Tomatoes, beans, corn, green peppers, red peppers, good and hot, and garlic, but no potatoes! *(walks into one store and buys tomatoes and corn, walks into another store and buys beans and garlic)* And the peppers? I'll get from Ricardo, our own Ricardo, at the store where he works. *(walks to a stand outside of another store)*

RICARDO: *(hurries out of the store to the little stand on the sidewalk)* Let me help you, Mamá! I hope you want something very good for our dinner tonight. I get hungry working here.

MAMÁ: Yes, Ricardo. For tonight, something special! *(reaches for the hot red peppers)* Mexicali Soup!

RICARDO: That's great. *(looks thoughtful)* But, Mamá—

MAMÁ: Yes? *(puts some peppers in her bag)*

RICARDO: Well, Mamá, you use a lot of hot peppers in your soup.

MAMÁ: *(smiles)* Of course.

RICARDO: A lot. *(pauses)* People here don't do that. They don't cook or eat the way we did at home in Mexico. I know, Mamá. I've worked here for weeks now. And in all that time, Mamá, I haven't sold as many hot peppers as you use in a week. Please don't put hot peppers in the soup, Mamá.

MAMÁ: No peppers. *(looks carefully at Ricardo)* Well, there are plenty of good things in the soup without peppers. I'll put more of something else. It will still make good soup.

RICARDO: *(puts the peppers back on the stand)* Of course, it will, Mamá. Everyone knows you make the best soup in the world.

MAMÁ: *(walks toward home)* Tomatoes, beans, garlic, corn. Yes, I can still make a good soup with those.

TOMÁS and RUBÉN: *(leave their game of stickball and run to Mamá)* Mamá!

TOMÁS: Oh, boy! Groceries! *(opens one bag)* Tomatoes and corn. I know what we're having for dinner.

RUBÉN: Me, too. *(looks into the other bag)* Beans and garlic. Mexicali Soup! Right, Mamá? *(looks thoughtful)* But, Mamá, listen.

MAMÁ: I'm listening.

RUBÉN: Well, I think we use an awful lot of beans. They don't use so many beans in the school lunch. You know, Mamá, they have different ways of doing things here. They're different from the ways of our town. I think we should try new ways. I think we shouldn't use so many beans. Mamá, please make Mexicali Soup without beans.

TOMÁS: Rubén is right. My teacher said only today that there's nothing that is so good that it cannot be made better, if we'll only try. I think there may be better ways of making soup than our old way. Make the soup tonight without tomatoes, Mamá!

MAMÁ: No tomatoes? And no beans? In Mexicali Soup? *(Mamá looks carefully at Tomás and Rubén and then closes the bags and walks away.)*

TOMÁS: We'll be hungry for your soup tonight, Mamá!

RUBÉN: Mamá! You make the best soup in the world!

MAMÁ: *(walks home and into her kitchen. Then takes the vegetables out of her bags)* No potatoes. No peppers. No tomatoes. No beans. Well, the soup will be a little thinner tonight.

ADELA: *(comes into the kitchen)* Hi, Mamá. I hope I'm in time. I heard you were making—*(looks at the groceries on the table)* All the way home I heard it. The boys and Teresa, they all told me. And Mamá, I want to ask you! Please, no garlic! Listen, Mamá. Last night, when my friend took me to dinner, I had such fine soup! The place was so beautiful, Mamá. And no garlic at all in the soup! Just leave out the garlic. You make the best soup in the world.

THE REST OF THE FAMILY: *(comes into the house)* Mamá! We're home, Mamá!

PAPÁ: *(walks into the kitchen with the others)* I heard something special. I heard we are having Mexicali Soup tonight. *(Mamá looks at Papá and says nothing.)* Your soup, Mamá, it's the best soup in the world.

MAMÁ: But you want me to leave out something? The corn, maybe? You want me to make my Mexicali Soup without the corn?

PAPÁ: Corn? *(opens his hands wide and shrugs)* What is corn? It is a little nothing. Put it in or leave it out. It doesn't matter. The soup will be just as—

MAMÁ: Enough! Out of here, all of you! *(waves her arms)* I have work to do. Go!

ADELA: But, Mamá, we always help you with—

MAMÁ: No! Out! *(The family goes into the living room and waits while Mamá fixes dinner.* MAMÁ *sings while she makes the soup and sets the table)* The soup is ready. Come and eat now.

PAPÁ: *(jumps up)* Ah! That's what I like to hear. The soup is ready before I have even started to smell it cooking.

TOMÁS and RUBÉN: *(running for the table)* Mmm-mmm!

TERESA, RICARDO, and ADELA: Mmm-mmm! Our Mamá makes the best soup in the world.

TERESA: *(looks at her bowl)* This doesn't look like Mexicali Soup.

TOMÁS: It doesn't smell like Mexicali Soup.

ADELA: *(puts her spoon down)* This isn't Mexicali Soup.   This is nothing but hot water!

PAPÁ: Did you forget to bring the soup, Mamá?

MAMÁ: *(smiles)* No.   This is the soup.   And it's just what you wanted.   I made the soup the way my family asked me to make it.   I left out the potatoes that Teresa doesn't want.   I left out the peppers that Ricardo doesn't want.   I left out the beans that Rubén doesn't want.   I left out the tomatoes that Tomás doesn't want.   For Adela, I left out the garlic.   And for Papá, I left out the corn, the little nothing that doesn't matter.   The new Mexicali Soup!   It's so quick!   So easy to make.   You just leave everything out of it.

Think About It

1. Why was Mamá so proud of her Mexicali Soup recipe?
2. Give the different reasons that Mamá's family asked her to leave out some of the ingredients.
3. How do you think Mamá felt about what her family asked her to do?
4. What lesson do you think Mamá's family learned?

Create and Share
Search in old magazines or cookbooks for a recipe that you think would taste awful. Then look for one that you think would taste good. Copy both recipes and share them in class.

Explore
This play is similar to the old folktale entitled "Stone Soup." Many authors have retold the folktale. Find and read a version of "Stone Soup."

Cloudy With a Chance of Meatballs

by Judi Barrett

We were all sitting around the big kitchen
table. It was Saturday morning. Pancake morning.
Mom was squeezing oranges for juice. Henry
and I were betting on how many pancakes we
each could eat. Grandpa was doing the flipping.

Seconds later, something flew through the air. It headed toward the kitchen ceiling . . . and landed right on Henry.

After we realized that the flying object was only a pancake, we all laughed, even Grandpa. All the other pancakes landed in the pan. And all of them were eaten, even the one that landed on Henry.

That night, touched off by the flying pancakes at breakfast, Grandpa told us the best tall-tale bedtime story he'd ever told.

Across an ocean, over lots of huge bumpy mountains, across three hot deserts, and one smaller ocean . . . there lay the tiny town of Chewandswallow. In most ways, it was very much like any other tiny town. It had a Main Street lined with stores, houses, gardens, a schoolhouse, about three hundred people, and some cats and dogs.

But there were no food stores in the town of Chewandswallow. The townspeople didn't need any. The sky supplied all the food they could want.

The only thing that was really different about Chewandswallow was its weather. It came three times a day—at breakfast, lunch, and dinner. Everything that everyone ate came from the sky. Whatever the weather served, that was what they ate.

But it never rained rain. It never snowed snow. And it never blew just wind. It rained things like soup and juice. It snowed mashed potatoes and green peas. And sometimes the wind blew in storms of hamburgers.

The people could watch the weather report on television. They would hear a prediction for the next day's food.

When the townspeople went outside, they carried their plates, cups, glasses, forks, spoons, knives and napkins with them. That way they would always be ready for any kind of weather. If there were leftovers the people took them home and put them in their refrigerators for snacks.

41

The menu was always different. By the time they woke up in the morning, breakfast was coming down. After a brief shower of orange juice, clouds of sunny-side-up eggs moved in followed by pieces of toast. Butter and jelly sprinkled down for the toast. And most of the time it rained milk afterward.

For lunch one day, hot dogs, already in their rolls, blew in from the northwest at about five miles an hour. There were mustard clouds nearby. Then the wind moved to the east and brought in baked beans. A drizzle of soda finished off the meal.

Dinner one night was lamb chops, becoming heavy at times, with occasional ketchup. Periods of peas and baked potatoes were followed by a wonderful Jell-O setting in the west.

The sanitation workers of Chewandswallow had a rather unusual job. They had to remove the food that fell on the houses and sidewalks and lawns. The workers cleaned things up after every meal and fed all the dogs and cats. Then they emptied some of it into the oceans for the fish and turtles and whales to eat. The rest of the food was put back into the earth. That made the soil richer for the people's flower gardens.

THE SANITATION
DEPARTMENT OF
CHEWANDSWALLOW

Life for the townspeople was delicious until the weather took a turn for the worse.

One day there was nothing but cheese all day long. The next day there was only broccoli, all overcooked. And the next day there were brussels sprouts and peanut butter with mayonnaise.

Another day there was a pea soup fog. No one could see where they were going and they could barely find the rest of the meal that got stuck in the fog.

The food was getting larger and larger. So was the amount of it. The people were getting frightened. Storms blew up often. Awful things were happening.

One Tuesday there was a hurricane of bread and rolls all day long. There were soft rolls and hard rolls, some with seeds and some without. There was white bread and rye and whole wheat toast. Most of it was larger than they had ever seen bread and rolls before. It was a terrible day. Everyone had to stay indoors. Roofs were damaged. The mess took the sanitation workers four days to clean up and the sea was full of floating rolls.

To help out, the people piled up as much bread as they could in their backyards. The birds picked at it a bit, but it just stayed there and got staler and staler.

There was a storm of pancakes one morning. Then came a downpour of maple syrup that nearly flooded the town. A huge pancake covered the school. No one could get it off because of its weight, so they had to close the school.

Lunch one day brought big drifts of cream cheese and jelly sandwiches. Everyone ate themselves sick and the day ended with a stomachache.

There was an awful salt and pepper wind followed by an even worse tomato tornado. People were sneezing themselves silly and running to avoid the tomatoes. The town was a mess. There were seeds and pulp everywhere.

The sanitation workers gave up. The job was too big. Everyone feared for their lives. They couldn't go outside most of the time. Many houses had been badly damaged by giant meatballs. Stores were boarded up and there was no more school for the children.

A decision was made to abandon the town of Chewandswallow. It was a matter of life and death.

The people glued together the giant pieces of stale bread sandwich-style with peanut butter.

The townspeople took only what they
absolutely needed with them. Then they set sail
on their rafts for a new land.

They floated for a week and finally reached a
small town, which welcomed them. The bread
had held up well. They built houses for
themselves out of it.

The children began school again, and the adults all tried to find places for themselves in the new land. The biggest change they had to make was getting used to buying food at the supermarket. They found it odd that the food was kept on shelves, packaged in boxes, cans and bottles. Meat that had to be cooked was kept in large refrigerators. Nothing came down from the sky except rain and snow. The clouds above their heads were not made of fried eggs. No one ever got hit by a hamburger again.

And nobody dared to go back to Chewandswallow to find out what had happened to it. They were too afraid.

Henry and I were awake until the very end of Grandpa's story. I remember his good-night kiss. The next morning we woke up to see snow falling outside our window. We ate breakfast a little faster than usual so we could go sledding with Grandpa. It's funny, but even as we were sliding down the hill we thought we saw a giant pat of butter at the top, and we could almost smell mashed potatoes.

Think About It

1. How do you know Grandpa's bedtime story is a tall tale?
2. Why is Chewandswallow a good name for the town in the story?
3. How did the change in weather affect the lives of the people in Chewandswallow?
4. How do changes in weather affect your life?
5. Why do you think the people from Chewandswallow are better off shopping at the supermarket?

Create and Share   Pretend you live in Chewandswallow. Draw a picture of yourself standing outside. Show a storm of your favorite meal and other foods you enjoy eating. Label the foods. Put your food storm up on the class bulletin board.

Explore   Investigate how weather is reported on television, on radio, and in newspapers. Share what you find out with your class.

Up, Up, and Away!

Up, up, and away
In my beautiful,
My beautiful balloon

*Words and Music
by Jimmy Webb*

Farmer Potter's Balloon Farm

a tall tale
by Jerdine Nolen

Harvey Potter was a very strange fellow indeed. He was a farmer, *but* he did not farm like my daddy did. He farmed a genuine government-inspected balloon farm.

No one knew exactly how he did it. Some folks say it wasn't real—that it was magic. But I know what I saw, and there were real actual balloons growing out of the ground!

He had some of the prettiest colors you'd ever want to see on a balloon. Pleasing purple, sun ray orange, yellin' yellow. There was rip two shot red, jelly bean black, blooming blue and grassy green. He had all kinds of balloon shapes too. Round ones. Long ones. Animal shapes. Clowns with big noses and mouths. He could even grow monster balloons, with scary faces and great big sharp teeth.

I tell you Harvey Potter was a strange fellow all right. To look at him, he was quite plain. But, the only thing that wasn't so plain about him was the stick he'd carry with him wherever he went. Sometimes he used it as a cane or walking stick. Mostly he just carried it under his arm.

55

It was Wheezle Mayfield who called the government on him in the first place. He said Harvey Potter was a health hazard. The government gave him the right to farm balloons. Before then, it was just plain unheard of to grow balloons. Ol' Wheezle, he was sore too.

  ~ The government came out to Harvey Potter's balloon farm bright and early one morning. Our whole town was there. Until that time, we never had balloons to play with. We all held our breath hoping we could keep our balloons. We never grew anything but trees—maple, sycamore, pine, and oak. We grew regular kinds of things like corn and okra and tomatoes and stuff like that. But Harvey Potter grew balloons. I'm telling you the way I know it. He grew them out of the plain old ground—and no one knew what he used for seed either.

Anyway, the government men and women, wearing white coats and white hats and white gloves, were standing around one of the balloons. They had roped us so far back we could hardly see, but I climbed up a sycamore tree and saw everything.

They pulled and they poked and finally they pricked a balloon with a pin. And what was supposed to happen did—the balloon popped.

Even they couldn't argue with that. So, the government gave him the right to grow balloons. Even though he never asked them for it, he took it anyway, just to be polite. Let me tell you, it made everybody happy. Well, almost everybody. Wheezle continued to be sore.

Now I had quite an interest in Harvey Potter's balloon farm myself. I decided I was going to get to know him, and I did. I'd bring him lemonade or sit on his porch and swing in his swing, but he never did confide in me about how he could do it. So, I didn't pry. After a while, I just liked being around him because he didn't ask questions about why this or why that. He just let a person sit and think out loud sometimes—and well, that's a good thing to do. But, something in me had to know how he did it. I decided I was just going to visit him some time and take a different kind of look around.

I do not know what made me go out there in the nighttime. Maybe it was because he did his field work at night. I told you he was strange.

I could see him very well. To this day, I am grateful to that sycamore tree, and the moon. It was as full as it was wide that night. I saw him the moment he opened his door.

He stood there on his front porch. His hands were inside his pockets. He was looking straight ahead where the fields were. He carried that big old stick under his arm. He waved it around over his head. He whomped and he hollered and he yelled and carried on so. *"EEeeeeeeee Ya-Ya-Yayayayaya, EeeeeeeeeeYaYaYaYa."* I am not ashamed to say, I was mighty scared. I was tempted to jump down and run home, but I just couldn't take my eyes off what he was doing. My eyes were just plain glued.

That stick of his started to bounce and float over the field. It was dropping down here and there in nice neat rows. All the while, Harvey Potter just kept whomping and screeching, *"EEeeeeeeee Ya-Ya-Yayayayaya, EeeeeeeeeeYaYaYaYa."*

All of a sudden, that stick came to a complete halt and flew back into his hand. That's when Harvey Potter stopped. He turned around, looking directly up at where I was hiding in that sycamore tree. I thought for sure he knew it was me. He must not have seen me though because he turned back around. He went back into his house for the rest of the night.

I climbed down and fell off to sleep, waiting. What for? To this day, I don't know.

61

In the morning, I woke up wet with dew and shivering-cold. I could see by the fresh light of day little-bitty colored mounds all over the ground. As I watched, they all came up in the glory of the day's sun. I tell you, it was a sight!

Harvey Potter saw me out there admiring them. He said I could take as many as I wanted—and I did! I took three, a clown, an elephant, and I just couldn't resist the jelly bean black one. I didn't touch the monster ones. They were just plain too scary.

I remember those days. It was the summer of '99. That was during the time I was getting ready to leave my home and find out what the world had to offer me. Harvey Potter grew me a balloon that was big enough to carry me far away from my home. That is how I landed in this place. I never did find my way back home and never did want to. I knew it was just right for me to be here. Farmer Potter never meant anyone any harm. He just grew the best and prettiest balloons this side of anywhere.

Now, as for me, I am not one to brag, but I have just harvested my 32nd crop of balloons. I don't grow mine the exact-same way Harvey Potter does, because I am not Harvey Potter. I have my own way. Perhaps I will show you how sometime.

Think About It

1. What makes "Farmer Potter's Balloon Farm" a tall tale?
2. Why is it fun to imagine a farm that has balloons growing in the fields?
3. If you were Farmer Potter, what would you do with your balloon crop?
4. In a tall tale, what other magical crop might grow on a farm?

Create and Share
Farmer Potter has given your class a small piece of land on his farm so you can grow your own special balloons. Draw a picture of your special balloon. It can be whatever you want—colorful, scary, or funny. Add yours to those of the rest of the class to make a balloon "crop."

Explore
Search for other tall tales to read. Retell one of these tales to the class.

The Red Balloon

from the book by Albert Lamorisse

Once upon a time in Paris there lived a little boy whose name was Pascal. He had no brothers or sisters, and he was very sad and lonely at home.

Once he brought home a lost cat, and some time later a stray puppy. But his mother said animals brought dirt into the house. Pascal was soon alone again in his mother's clean house.

One day, on his way to school, Pascal caught sight of a fine red balloon tied to a street lamp. He laid his school bag on the ground. He climbed up the lamppost, untied the balloon, and ran off with it to the bus stop.

But the driver knew the rules. "No dogs," he said. "No large packages, no balloons."

People with dogs walk. People with packages take taxis. People with balloons leave them behind.

Pascal did not want to leave his balloon behind, so the driver rang the signal bell and the bus went on without him.

Pascal's school was a long way off. When he finally reached the school door, it was already shut. To be late for school and with a balloon— that was unheard of! Pascal was very worried.

He had an idea. He left his balloon with the janitor, who was sweeping the yard.

When school was over, the janitor gave it back to him. Pascal had to walk home because of those silly rules about balloons on buses.

His mother was glad to see him finally come home. She had been very worried. She was angry when she found out that it was a balloon that had made Pascal late. She took the balloon, opened the window, and threw it out.

Now, usually when you let a balloon go, it flies away. But Pascal's balloon stayed outside the window, and the two of them looked at each other through the glass. Pascal was surprised that his balloon hadn't flown away, but not really as surprised as all that. Friends will do all kinds of things for you. If the friend is a balloon, it doesn't fly away. So Pascal opened his window and took his balloon back inside.

The next day, before he left for school, Pascal opened the window to let his balloon out. He told it to come to him when he called. Then he picked up his school bag, kissed his mother good-by, and went downstairs.

When he reached the street, he called, "Balloon! Balloon!" The balloon came flying down to him. Then it began to follow Pascal— without being led by a string, just as if it were a dog following its master.

But, like a dog, it didn't always do as it was told. When Pascal tried to catch it to cross the street, the balloon flew beyond his reach. Pascal decided to pretend he didn't care. He walked up the street just as if the balloon weren't there at all and hid behind the corner of a house. The balloon got worried and hurried to catch up with him.

When they got to the bus stop, Pascal said to the balloon: "Now, Balloon, you follow me. Don't lose sight of the bus!" That was how the strangest sight came to be seen in a Paris street— a balloon flying along behind a bus.

When they reached Pascal's school, the balloon again tried not to be caught. The bell was already ringing and the door was just about to close, so Pascal had to hurry in alone. He was very worried.

Pascal saw the balloon fly in the window. Next, the balloon got in line behind the children. The teacher was very surprised to see this strange new pupil. When the balloon tried to follow them into the classroom, the children made so much noise that the principal came along to see what was happening.

The principal tried to catch the balloon to put it out the door. But he couldn't. Instead, he took Pascal by the hand and marched him out of class.

The balloon left the classroom and followed them. Pascal had to spend the rest of the day in the principal's office. The balloon followed the principal around all day. The poor man tried very hard to catch the balloon, but he couldn't, so there was nothing to do but put up with it.

At the end of the day, the principal was only too glad to let Pascal out of his office, and to be rid of him and his balloon. On the way home Pascal stopped to look at a picture in a sidewalk exhibit.

69

At that very moment some of the tough boys of the neighborhood came by. They tried to catch the balloon as it trailed along behind Pascal. But the balloon saw the danger. It flew to Pascal at once. Pascal caught it and began to run, but more boys came to corner him from the other side.

So Pascal let go of his balloon, which immediately rose high into the sky. While the boys were all looking up, Pascal ran between them to the top of the steps. From there he called his balloon, which came to him at once—to the great surprise of the boys in the gang. Then Pascal went into a bakeshop for some cake. Before he went inside, he said to the balloon: "Now be good and wait for me. Don't go away."

The balloon was good and only went as far as the corner of the shop to warm itself in the sun; but that was already too far because the gang of boys saw it. Without being seen they crept up to it, jumped on it and carried it away.

When Pascal came out of the bakeshop, there was no balloon! He ran in every direction, looking up at the sky. The balloon had disobeyed him again! It had gone off by itself! And although he called at the top of his voice, the balloon did not come back.

The gang had tied the balloon to a strong
string, and they were trying to teach it tricks.
"We could show this magic balloon in a circus,"
one of them said. He shook a stick at the
balloon. "Come here or I'll burst you," he
shouted.

Pascal saw the balloon over the top of a wall,
desperately dragging at the end of its heavy
string. He called to it. As soon as it heard his
voice, the balloon flew toward him. Pascal
quickly untied the string and ran off with his
balloon as fast as he could run.

The boys raced after them. They made so
much noise that everyone in the neighborhood
stopped to watch the chase. It seemed as if
Pascal had stolen the boys' balloon. Pascal
thought, "I'll hide in the crowd." But a red
balloon can be seen anywhere, even in a crowd.

Pascal ran through
narrow alleys, trying to
lose the gang of boys.

At one point the boys
didn't know whether
Pascal had turned
right or left, so they
split up into several
groups. For a
minute Pascal

thought he had escaped them, and he looked around for a place to rest. But as he rounded a corner, he bumped right into one of the gang. He ran back the way he had come, but there were more boys there. He was desperate—he ran up a side street which led to an empty lot. He thought he'd be safe there.

But suddenly boys appeared from every direction, and Pascal was surrounded. So he let go of his balloon. This time, instead of chasing the balloon, the gang attacked Pascal. The balloon flew a little way off, but when it saw Pascal fighting, it came back. The boys began throwing stones at the balloon.

"Fly away, Balloon! Fly away!" Pascal cried. But the balloon would not leave its friend.

Then one stone hit the balloon, and it burst.

While Pascal was crying over his dead balloon, the strangest thing happened! Everywhere balloons could be seen flying up into the air and forming a line high into the sky.

All the balloons of Paris came down to Pascal, dancing around him, twisting their strings into one strong one and lifting him up into the sky. And that was how Pascal took a wonderful trip all around the world.

Think About It

1. Why was the red balloon so special to Pascal?
2. Tell about the problems the balloon made for Pascal.
3. Could there really be a balloon like the one in this story? Why or why not?
4. How did you feel when the stone popped the balloon?
5. What could you learn from this story?

Create and Share   Imagine that you have your own red balloon. What kind of magic would you want your red balloon to have? What adventures might you have with your balloon? Draw pictures and describe your experiences.

Explore   Find another story or book to read about a toy that is magical.

The Rise and Fall and Rise of Ballooning

by Hal Ober

Many of you probably saw a hot-air balloon for the first time in an adventure story or a movie. Balloons are an old-fashioned way to fly, but now ballooning is enjoyed as a sport.

Over 200 years ago, two French brothers, the Montgolfiers, noticed the way bits of paper floated above a fire. They knew that when air is hot, it becomes lighter and it rises. If that hot air is inside a bag or balloon, the bag or balloon will rise with it.

On September 19, 1783, the Montgolfiers launched a large balloon. It was made of cloth and paper and filled with hot smoke. Three passengers went along for the ride—a duck, a rooster, and a sheep. Two months later two people went up in a balloon. They flew five miles over Paris, France.

People then began building bigger balloons and taking longer rides. Hot-air balloons were good for short, quick climbs. There were also balloons filled with a very light gas called hydrogen. They flew even farther.

In 1906, a newspaper publisher, Gordon Bennett, held a big race for hot-air balloons in Paris. (An American won it by flying nearly 400 miles, to England.) Soon, though, the age of the balloon turned into the age of the airplane.

In the 1960's, the old hobby of ballooning got a big lift. A new way to heat the air in the balloon was invented. The air was heated by a small propane gas burner. Just by turning up the heat, the pilot could make the balloon rise higher. To make it go down, the pilot only had to open a long, narrow vent in the side of the balloon. This vent let some of the hot air escape.

Many people began to see ballooning as something they could do too. Ballooning festivals began popping up in places like New York, South Carolina, and New Mexico. Every year thousands of people now flock to balloon festivals to watch the colorful balloons fill the sky. Each year more and more people take up the hobby of hot-air ballooning.

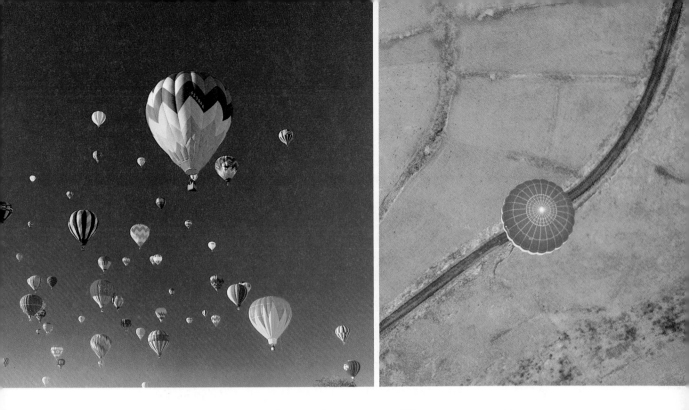

Just how do these hot-air balloons get off the
ground? Early morning is the best time for hot-air
balloons to rise, when the winds are lightest. The
empty balloon is spread out on the ground. By
using a fan or flapping the material up and down,
the crew makes a bubble of air inside. Then
the pilot heats the air with the burner until the
balloon stands up straight and full, ready to go.

Dozens of balloons lift off, rising until they
find a breeze that is blowing in the direction they
want to go. At many festivals, there are balloon
races, balloon chases, and target events like the
Key Grab. In the Key Grab, the pilot tries to fly
near a pole and grab a set of keys (to a prize car).
Of course there are always balloon rides for
young and old.

Let's not forget gas balloons. They are usually filled with helium—the same gas that makes party balloons fly away. These balloons too are spread out on the ground. Then gas, not hot air, is pumped into them until they are ready to go. They are more expensive than the average hot-air balloon, but helium goes much farther than hot air. In 1978 three balloonists crossed the Atlantic Ocean, over 3,000 miles, in their helium balloon, *Double Eagle II*. In 1981, *Double Eagle V* flew across the Pacific Ocean, 5,208 miles, from Japan to California.

One famous balloonist, Malcolm Forbes, says, "There's no quicker way of getting to know people than to drop in on them out of the sky in a balloon." The hobby of ballooning is on the rise, not because it is a faster way to travel, but because it's slower—ballooning takes time and brings people together.

Think About It

1. What would be scary about flying in a balloon?
2. What would be wonderful about flying in a balloon?
3. How has ballooning changed since the days of the Montgolfier brothers?
4. What important things do you need to know before you launch a balloon for a ride?
5. Why do you think so many people are going to balloon festivals?

Create and Share

Imagine that you are up in a balloon. Draw a picture of your school or neighborhood as it might look from above.

Explore

Find out more about the history of ballooning. Look for books that tell how it got started and where it is most popular.

How the Balloon

Was Launched

from THE WIZARD OF OZ
by L. Frank Baum

For three days Dorothy heard nothing from Oz. These were sad days for the little girl, although her friends were all quite happy. The Scarecrow told them there were wonderful thoughts in his head. He would not say what they were because he knew no one could understand them but himself. When the Tin Woodman walked about he felt his heart rattling around. He told Dorothy it was a kinder and more tender heart than the one he had owned when he was made of flesh. The Lion declared he was afraid of nothing on earth, and would gladly face an army of men.

Thus each of the little party was happy except Dorothy, who longed more than ever to get back to Kansas.

On the fourth day, to her great joy, Oz sent for her. When she entered the Throne Room he said, pleasantly:

"Sit down, my dear. I think I have found the way to get you out of this country."

"And back to Kansas?" she asked eagerly.

"Well, I'm not sure about Kansas," said Oz, "for I haven't the faintest idea which way it lies. But the first thing to do is to cross the desert, and then it should be easy to find your way home."

"How can I cross the desert?" she asked.

"Well, I'll tell you what I think," said the little man. "You see, when I came to this country it was in a balloon. You also came through the air, being carried by a cyclone. So I believe the best way to get across the desert will be through the air. Now, it is quite beyond my powers to make a cyclone; but I've been thinking the matter over, and I believe I can make my old balloon fly again."

"How?" asked Dorothy.

"A balloon," said Oz, "is made of silk, which is coated with glue to keep the gas in it. But in all this country there is no gas to fill the balloon with, to make it float."

"If it won't float," said Dorothy, "it will be of no use to us."

"True," answered Oz. "But there is another way to make it float, which is to fill it with hot air. Hot air isn't as good as gas, for if the air should get cold the balloon would come down in the desert, and we should be lost."

"We!" said Dorothy. "Are you going with me?"

"Yes, of course," replied Oz. "I am tired of being such a humbug. If I should go out of this Palace my people would soon discover I am not a Wizard. Then they would be mad at me for having fooled them. So I have to stay shut up in these rooms all day, and it gets tiresome. I'd much rather go back to Kansas with you and be in a circus again."

"I shall be glad to have your company," said Dorothy.

"Thank you," he answered.

Oz sent word to his people that he was going to make a visit to a great brother Wizard who lived in the clouds. The news spread rapidly throughout the city and everyone came to see the wonderful sight.

Oz ordered the balloon carried out in front of the Palace, and the people gazed upon it with much curiosity. The Tin Woodman had chopped a big pile of wood, and now he made a fire of it, and Oz held the bottom of the balloon over the fire so that the hot air that arose from it would be caught in the silken bag. Slowly the balloon swelled out and rose into the air, until finally the basket just touched the ground.

Then Oz got into the basket and said to all the people in a loud voice:

"I am now going away to make a visit. While I am gone the Scarecrow will rule over you. I command you to obey him as you would me."

The balloon was by this time tugging hard at the rope that held it to the ground. The air within it was hot, and this made it so much lighter in weight than the air without that it pulled hard to rise into the sky.

"Come, Dorothy!" cried the Wizard. "Hurry up, or the balloon will fly away."

"I can't find Toto anywhere," yelled Dorothy, who did not wish to leave her little dog behind. Toto had run into the crowd to bark at a kitten. Dorothy at last found him. She picked him up and ran toward the balloon.

She was within a few steps of it, and Oz was holding out his hands to help her into the basket, when, crack! went the ropes. The balloon rose into the air without her.

"Come back!" she screamed. "I want to go too!"

"I can't come back, my dear," called Oz from the basket. "Good-bye."

"Good-bye!" shouted everyone, and all eyes were turned upward to where the Wizard was riding in the basket, rising every moment farther and farther into the sky.

And that was the last any of them ever saw of Oz, the Wonderful Wizard. But all the people remembered him lovingly.

What about poor Dorothy? What about poor Toto? Do they have to stay in Oz forever? Don't worry. They missed a wonderful balloon ride back to Kansas, but they do get home . . . somehow.

Think About It

1. Why is Dorothy unhappy in the story?
2. Describe how Oz says he will help Dorothy.
3. Tell what goes wrong with Oz's plan for the balloon trip.
4. Do you think Dorothy may have been better off missing the balloon? Why or why not?

Create and Share   Where do you think the balloon carried the Wizard? Write about what happens to the Wizard on his balloon ride.

Explore   This story is part of *The Wizard of Oz*, by L. Frank Baum. Read the whole book for more about Dorothy's adventures.

There once was a panda named Lou
Who only liked crunching bamboo.
He ate all day long
Till he looked like King Kong.
Now the zoo doesn't know what to do.

Pandas

Once There Were No Pandas

a Chinese legend
retold by Margaret Greaves

Long, long ago in China, when the earth and stars were young, there were none of the black-and-white bears that the Chinese call *xiong mao* and that we call pandas. But deep in the bamboo forests lived bears with fur as white and soft as snow. The Chinese called them *bai xiong*, which means "white bear."

In a small house at the edge of the forest lived a peasant and his wife. They had a little daughter, Chien-min.

One very hot day, Chien-min was playing alone at the edge of the forest. She saw a patch of beautiful yellow buttercups.

"They are only *just* inside the forest," said the little girl to herself. "It will take only a minute to pick some."

She slipped in among the trees. But when she had picked her flowers, she looked around, puzzled. There were so many small paths! Which one led back to the village?

As she hesitated, something moved among the leaves nearby. It was one of the small deer of the forest. Chien-min had scared it, and it ran away between the trees. She tried to follow, hoping it might lead her home. But almost at once it was out of sight. Now Chien-min was completely lost.

She began to be frightened. Then she heard another sound. Something was whimpering not far away. She ran toward the place, forgetting her fear, wanting only to help.

There, close to a big thorny bush, sat a very small white bear cub. Every now and then he shook one of his front paws and licked it. Then he whimpered again.

"Oh, you poor little one!" said Chien-min. She ran over and knelt beside the little bear. "Don't cry! I'll help you. Let me see it."

The cub seemed to understand. He let her take hold of his paw. Between the pads was a very sharp thorn. Chien-min pinched it between her finger and thumb. Very carefully she drew it out. The cub rubbed his head against her hands as she stroked him.

A moment later, a huge white bear came crashing through the trees, growling fiercely. When she saw that the little girl was only playing with her cub, her anger disappeared. She licked his paw, then nuzzled Chien-min as if she too were one of her cubs.

The mother bear was so gentle that Chien-min
took courage. She put her arms round the
mother bear's neck, stroking the soft fur. "How
beautiful you are!" she said. "Oh, if only you
could show me the way home."

At once the great bear walked forward. She grunted to the cub and his new friend to follow. Fearlessly now, Chien-min held on to the thick white coat. She soon found that she was at the edge of the forest again, close to her own home.

From that day on, she often went into the forest. Her parents were happy about it, knowing their daughter was safe under the protection of the great white bear. She met many of the other bears, too, and many of their young. But her special friend was always the little cub she had helped. She called him Niao Niao, which means "very soft," because his fur was so fine and beautiful.

The mother bear showed the little girl her secret home, a den in the hollow of a great tree. Chien-min went there many times, played with the cubs, and learned the ways of the forest. Always the great she-bear led her safely back before nightfall.

One warm spring afternoon, Chien-min was sitting by the hollow tree, watching the cubs at play. She saw a movement between the bamboos. A wide, whiskered face. Fierce topaz eyes. Small tufted ears. A glimpse of spotted, silky fur.

Chien-min sprang up, shouting a warning. But she was too late. With bared teeth and lashing tail, the hungry leopard had leaped upon Niao Niao.

Chien-min forgot all fear in her love for her friend. Snatching up a great stone, she hurled it at the leopard. The leopard dropped his prey but turned on her, snarling with fury. At the same moment, the she-bear charged through the trees like a thunderbolt.

The leopard backed off, terrified by her anger. As he turned to run, he struck out at Chien-min with his huge claws, knocking her to the ground.

The bears ran to Chien-min, growling and whining and licking her face. But the little girl never moved. She had saved Niao Niao's life by the loss of her own.

News of her death swept through the forest. From miles away, north, south, east and west, all the white bears gathered to mourn. They wept and whimpered for their lost friend. They rubbed their paws in the dust of the earth and wiped the tears from their eyes. As they did so, the wet dust left great black smears across their faces. They beat their paws against their bodies in sadness. When they did this, the wet dust clung to their fur in wide black bands.

The bears and Chien-min's parents mourned her. But they were all comforted to know that she was happy. Guan-yin, the Goddess of Mercy, would reward her for her selfless love for her friend.

From that day to this, there have been no white bears, *bai xiong*, anywhere in China. Instead there are the great black-and-white bears, *xiong mao*, that we call pandas, still mourning for their lost friend, Chien-min.

Think About It

1. How did Chien-min become a special friend of the great white bears?
2. What made Chien-min come to Niao Niao's rescue?
3. How did the bears show their love of Chien-min?
4. Tell how the story made you feel.

Create and Share   Use your imagination to write a legend that explains how the leopard got its spots. Share your stories.

Explore   Search for other stories that tell why animals look the way they do. Rudyard Kipling is the author who wrote *Just So* stories. Ananse folktales from Africa explain why spiders look the way they do. Read some of these stories and share them with your class. You may even find one about the leopard that you can compare to the one you wrote.

PANDAS

by Katherine Talmadge, Susan DeStefano, and
Elizabeth West

Giant pandas are large black-and-white
animals that look like teddy bears. They grow to
be about 5 feet long. They can weigh up to 200
pounds. The black furry circles around their
eyes make them look a little sad.

A newborn panda doesn't look very special.
It weighs less than half a pound and doesn't look
at all like its mother. It looks more like a hairless
pink mouse. Panda babies are born totally
helpless. Their eyes are shut, and they have no
fur to keep them warm. Like all mammals, they
need milk from their mother to survive. They
also need protection from leopards and other
wild animals.

Pandas spend more than half of each day eating. They eat a huge amount of bamboo—up to 40 pounds a day. Bamboo is a kind of wild grass. It grows tall and tough like a tree. When pandas eat bamboo, they sit down like a human being at a picnic. They hold the sticks of bamboo in their paws. Then they push the tough branches of bamboo into their mouths and use their powerful jaws and teeth to grind up the branches.

The fact that pandas sit up in such a funny human pose when they eat is puzzling. Some scientists believe that pandas are relatives of bears, but bears do not eat like this. Other scientists think that pandas belong to the same animal family as raccoons, but raccoons don't eat like pandas either.

Whatever they are, pandas are cute and very popular. Sadly, they are also rare. They are endangered animals. This means that only a small number still live in the wild. Those pandas live in the country of China. People fear that one day in the future, there will be no more pandas.

Pandas are endangered for many reasons. To survive, they must live where their food grows. In one area of China, the weather changed and the bamboo stopped growing. In other places in China, people cut down the bamboo trees to clear the land. Many pandas died because there wasn't enough bamboo.

There is another reason why so few pandas live in the wild. Unlike dogs and cats, pandas usually have only one baby at a time. This means it takes a long time for the number of pandas to increase.

KEY
- ▮ Panda Range
- • Panda Reserves

Beijing
(Peking)

East
China Sea

CHINA

Hong Kong

South China Sea

N
W   E
S

The people of China want to protect their pandas and help them increase in number. The Chinese have made safety areas called panda reserves in the mountains. This is where most wild pandas now live. In these reserves, the pandas are free to wander through dense forests of bamboo.

The people of China have made the panda the symbol of their country. They have made laws against hurting the pandas. Also, they don't let people take pandas out of China. Not many zoos have been able to get a panda, so many people outside of China have never seen one.

The United States is lucky. The people of China offered the United States two giant pandas, and the United States was thankful for these gifts. The pandas live in the National Zoo in Washington, D.C. People travel from all over the country to see them.

Pandas are fun to watch. They do somersaults, and they play with plastic balls and hoops. They splash in their bath. And they eat, eat, eat! The pandas at the National Zoo are popular with zoo visitors of all ages.

That was the idea the people of China had when they gave the pandas to the United States. China hopes that more people will get to see them so that more people will want to help save the pandas there. The idea has worked!

Now a group called the World Wildlife Fund is
helping to save the pandas. It is studying wild
pandas and the type of farming that is needed to
grow bamboo. Scientists in countries all over the
world are working hard to learn more about
pandas so they can help them. The future of the
panda depends on what these people find out.
No one wants these cuddly animals to disappear.

Think About It

1. Name some important things you learned about pandas from this article that you did not know before.
2. Can you tell from this article if the authors want to protect pandas? Explain.
3. How do you know that the Chinese government cares about pandas?
4. Why should endangered animals like the panda be helped?

Create and Share   Make a poster about saving the panda. What pictures and messages will you put on it?

Explore   Use a map or globe to locate the area in China where pandas live.

I Find Su-lin

by Ruth Harkness

Ruth Harkness was the first person to bring a live giant panda to America. Her husband died while searching for a giant panda in China in 1935. Ruth took over his expedition.

Helped by a Chinese guide named Quentin Young and several others, she traveled across China and into the mountainous jungle where giant pandas lived.

This is Ruth's own story of what happened.

Quentin

Ruth

We climbed up the steep, wet mountainside.
The bamboo jungle was so thick we could barely
get through it. I wondered how big animals like
pandas could slip through the jungle without a
great deal of noise. Our hunters said that even
the big pandas are very shy. They said they
could disappear as quietly as smoke.

The bamboo was like a shower. There had
been rain and snow the night before. We hadn't
gone very far before we were drenched to the
skin and panting for breath. The clouds hung
far down into the valleys. Soon we were right
in the middle of them.

Quentin showed me the first trap. It was a little hole in the ground, just big enough for a panda's foot. It had a little loop of rope hidden under the dead leaves. When the panda's foot stepped into this hole, a small tree with a wire attached would snap up. We were very careful to set only the kind of traps that could never injure an animal. Only once have I seen an animal caught in a cruel trap. I have never forgotten it.

A little farther on we looked at another trap. I tried to imagine what we'd do if we found a big panda in it. The stuffed ones I had seen in museums had very long, pointed claws. They also had very sharp teeth for chewing the tough bamboo.

If we were to find a full-grown panda in one of our traps, we would have a great problem. His claws and teeth wouldn't be out of reach of anyone who tried to tie him. Our hunters would have to go back to camp and build some kind of cage. But how would we get a giant panda in it? Then how would we get the whole business down the steep mountainside? I could hardly get down myself without sliding most of the way.

I began to wonder if I really wanted a panda. I knew I'd feel so sorry for him. After a while I'd want to let him go back to the jungles he loved, safe from human beings.

Quentin

Ruth

after the shot.

The jungle was so thick, I couldn't see two feet before me. When a shot rang out ahead of us, I didn't know for a few moments what had happened. I heard the hunters shouting and Quentin calling out orders in Chinese. I knew it must be something exciting and I pushed ahead as fast as I could. After falling and slipping, I came up to Quentin. He told me that the hunters had caught a glimpse of a big panda. They shouldn't have fired at it, for we didn't want a dead panda. I was delighted when we discovered that it had not been hit.

We plowed on a little farther through the dripping bamboo. Quentin stopped suddenly. He listened a moment and then went forward so rapidly I couldn't keep up with him. Through the wet branches, I saw him standing near a huge rotting tree. I followed as best I could, brushing the water from my face and eyes. Then I, too, stopped—frozen in my tracks.

From the old dead tree trunk came a baby's whimper.

Perhaps an abandoned Chinese baby? No, that couldn't be possible in this forest so far from the places where people lived.

Quentin reaches for
whimpering baby

Quentin reached into the hollow trunk of the tree. Then he turned and walked toward me. In his arms was a *baby*. It was a baby who was whimpering just as your own little brother or sister might. But it wasn't any kind of baby you or I had ever seen before. It was a baby giant panda.

weight
2 pounds

I took her in my hands. She wasn't any bigger than a kitten, and just as blind as newborn kittens are. She looked exactly like a tiny picture of the big stuffed pandas I had seen in museums. The panda I held in my hands weighed perhaps two pounds. I had thought I would find something fierce, weighing three hundred pounds or more! Quentin and the other hunters agreed that she couldn't be more than ten days old.

The little animal nuzzled in my coat. She was too tiny, too newly born to know that I wasn't her mother. She was hungry, and the little cry was just like a real baby's cry. It was sad. I had brought a baby's bottle and dried milk on the trip, but they were in the camp far down the valley. We had to hurry back immediately.

Quentin tucked the baby inside his shirt. She finally went to sleep, and as fast as we could we went back down the mountain. It seemed as though we would never get there. Whenever she woke, our little baby cried for food.

Quentin and baby

By late afternoon we arrived in camp. Quentin hurriedly mixed some dried milk with warm water. Then I held the baby panda in my arms and fed her from a bottle. It was just like feeding a tiny human baby.

Next we made her a cradle out of one of the cases we used to carry our clothes and food. We lined the cradle with a shirt, and hung it from a pole in the tent. The baby panda was now warm and well-fed. She waved her paws a few times, made funny little happy noises in her throat, and went to sleep.

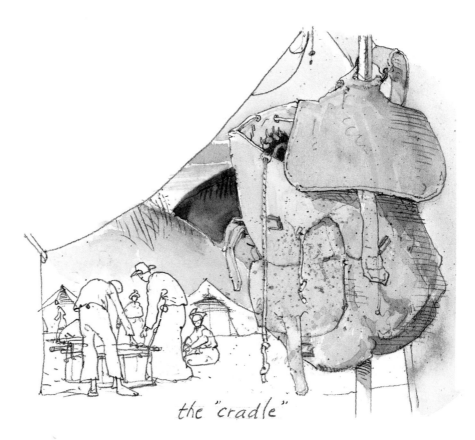

the "cradle"

Then we sat down to talk about what to do next. I wanted to stay in our little camp and watch the baby panda grow up in that lovely valley. I couldn't imagine anything that would have been more fun, but Quentin said no. After all, we didn't have much dried milk with us, and only one bottle. What would we do if it ever got broken? In those mountains of far western China there were no grocery stores. Even if we had traveled for many days to the nearest big town, we wouldn't have been able to buy milk for her.

So we decided that we would pack up as soon as we could and journey down the mountains to the nearest big city, Chengtu. From there the panda and I could fly to Shanghai, where we would get a boat to the United States.

Within two days we realized that it would be much easier to raise a human baby than a baby giant panda. We called her Su-lin, because that means "a little bit of something very precious." But even "something very precious" can be hungry. Su-lin wanted to be fed at all hours— even two o'clock in the morning when it was cold and rainy. Sometimes she'd wake up in the middle of the night and be chilly or just lonesome for her mother, so I would take her into bed with me. After all, I was sorry to have taken her from the mother panda our hunters had frightened away.

Ruth and Su-lin

I wanted to make it up to her. She would
cry a little and then snuggle down in my hair
and go to sleep.

There was also the problem of keeping her
cradle dry. We used my shirts and Quentin's
sweater—everything we had, which wasn't very
much. That was the one thing I hadn't thought
of. All babies need changes of blankets and
such. We finally tore up a few towels we had and
tried to put diapers on her. She squirmed and
wiggled and finally yipped at us. She would
have none of it.

Whang, one of our hunters, made a little basket of bamboo for Su-lin to travel in. I put my big shaggy gray blanket in the basket. Then we tucked in Su-lin herself. When we were ready to start, another of our hunters strapped the basket on his back, and off we set. Su-lin, Quentin and I, with several hunters, started on the long trip that was to end in America. It was surely one of the strangest trips ever made. The important figure in our trip was the first giant panda ever captured alive. At the moment she was a very small giant, indeed.

Think About It

1. Why did Ruth Harkness want to take a live panda to the United States?
2. How do you know that Ruth Harkness is a very kind and caring hunter?
3. What do you think happened to the baby panda in the United States?
4. Why do you think the author wrote this story?
5. Tell what new things you learned about pandas from reading these stories in PANDAS.

Create and Share   If you were a reporter for a magazine and could interview Ruth Harkness when she arrives in the United States with Su-lin, what four questions would you ask? Write your questions. Work with a partner and take turns interviewing each other.

Explore   Search for information about any zoos in the United States that have pandas. Start your search by looking up the National Zoo in Washington, D.C.

My Pen Pal

That's Write!

Pigs cannot write poems because
Nothing rhymes with *oink*. If you
Think you can find a rhyme, I'll pause,
But if I wait until you do,
I'll have forgotten why it was
Pigs cannot write poems because.

WHY PIGS CANNOT WRITE POEMS
by John Ciardi

Dear Aunt Helen

by Helen S. Munro

"What does Miss Touchin think I am—a robot?" muttered Joseph as he trudged home from school. "Write, write, write. First a report on snails, then Indians. Now she wants me to write letters to some old lady in a retirement home. I'll have to waste my whole weekend trying to think of what to say to someone I don't even know!"

Joseph let himself in the front door and dropped his book bag with a thump. He headed for the cookie tin that his grandmother had sent from Italy. Scooping up his baseball and glove, he ran out the back door with a handful of cookies. First he'd play ball with his friends. The letter could wait till Sunday.

A light was on in the kitchen, and the delicious smell of spaghetti sauce greeted him when he came home for supper.

"Hi, Joseph. Dinner is ready." His mother turned as he came into the kitchen. He ducked under her arm, and her welcoming kiss just missed its mark. Ever since his father had gone back to Italy to see the grandparents and sell the family stone-carving business, Joseph's mother seemed to kiss him a lot.

Joseph was hungry, and the spaghetti tasted great. "Supper was really good, Mom," he told her as he helped with the dishes. He liked working in the kitchen. Cooking was fun, and he didn't even mind cleaning up.

"As your father would say, some of us are lucky enough to be born Italian. Everybody else just eats Italian." His mother laughed as she folded her apron. "Well, now, how much homework do you have for Monday? We'll be busy at the shop tomorrow, and we're going to Uncle Antonio's farm on Sunday, so you better do your lessons tonight!"

Rats, thought Joseph, I can't even put it off until Sunday. Out loud he said, "Just a letter for English."

"Then get to it," answered his mother.

The moment had come. He got out his pencil and paper and looked at the name: *Mrs. Helen Smith.* Might as well get it over with.

Dear Mrs. Smith,

My name is Joseph, and I am nine years old. I am in the third grade. I would like to be your pen pal.

Sincerely,
Joseph Bellini

That says it all. How much more would an old lady want to know about a little kid, thought Joseph. Especially me.

The weekend went quickly. On Monday Miss Touchin found only one mistake in Joseph's letter. He copied it over in his neatest handwriting, mailed it, and forgot about it.

About a week later, Joseph found a letter in the mailbox, addressed to Master Joseph Bellini. "That's me!" he shouted —and tore it open immediately.

Dear Joseph,

   I am eighty-one years old and not in the third grade. I live in a retirement home with a lot of other ladies. Our building is all on one floor, and my room has a door that goes outside to a small patio. I planted petunias today, and I'm going to invite everyone to a party in my petunia patch.

   The ladies here are nice but a little dull. What do you do for fun?

Sincerely,
H. Smith

P.S. Please call me Aunt Helen, as my nieces, great-nieces and nephews and friends do. Mrs. Smith sounds like the name of a pie!

Joseph was excited about his letter and took it to school the next day. What a mistake!

"Well, write her another letter," said Miss Touchin. "Show it to me before you send it, and I'll give you some extra credit in English for it."

Rats and double rats, more writing, thought Joseph. But somehow Aunt Helen sounded better than Mrs. Smith.

Dear Aunt Helen,

I'm glad you are out of the third grade. I wish I were.

My baseball team finally won a game. I hit the ball, and a dog grabbed it and ran away. I scored the only run, and without the ball we couldn't play.

Sincerely, your pen pal,
Joseph

P.S. That's what I do for fun. Baseball, not school.

Another week went by, and another letter arrived.

Dear Joseph,

I'm glad to hear that your team won, sneaky as it was.

Some of the ladies here feel about this place as you feel about school. Their children put them here. I have passed out all the lipsticks I got for presents to try to make them look cheerier.

I feel that I am lucky. My husband and I had no children, and I am here because it is a good place for me. I get three meals a day, and when they have liver, they don't make me eat it.

Love, your friend,
Aunt Helen

131

This time Joseph got smart and didn't show it
to his teacher. But somehow he still felt like writing.

Dear Aunt Helen,

Thanks for the letter. My mom got a
letter today, too. My dad is in Italy, and
my grandfather died. Now I have just my
grandma, who will come to live with us.
My mom cried and cried.

How are you? Do you think dying hurts?

Love, your friend,
Joseph

Dear Joseph,

    I've been so busy living, Joseph, that I don't know if dying hurts or not. My husband was in pain one moment and died the next. His face looked young and peaceful and definitely without pain.

    My pain after he died was great, and I guess I can say that death is not painful but living can be. Give your mom a hug. It helps the hurt.

Love,
Aunt Helen

When his mom got home that night, Joseph was in the kitchen. He had salad making down pat from helping his mother. He had just finished reading the directions for making a "puffy omelet." He separated the eggs and then whipped the egg whites until he thought his arm would fall off. After carefully putting them together, he poured what he was sure was a mess into the hot, buttered pan. To his surprise, the omelet puffed up just as the cookbook had said it would.

His mother was amazed. "Thank you, Joseph." She seemed to laugh and cry at the same time. "Great news! We're picking up Dad and Grandma at the airport tonight!"

The plane was fifteen minutes late. Joseph fidgeted until it landed. His dad came down the ramp looking tired and somehow smaller than Joseph remembered. Holding onto his arm was a black-haired lady with sad eyes.

Joseph and his grandmother became friends in no time. In a few days he was teaching her English, and she helped him with his Italian. Sometimes he sounded just like his teacher: "Now try it again. You'll get it."

His letter to Aunt Helen that week was a little longer than usual.

Dear Aunt Helen,

My grandmother is sixty-one, but her English is about third grade. I think she must look like you. Let me know when your petunia patch blooms, and we'll come to see you. My teacher says my writing has really improved. When she asked who has been helping me, I said, "Aunt Helen." She gave me a strange look. She knows my family. I never told her that we are still pen pals. Every boy needs at least one secret, and I guess you're mine.

Love,
Joseph

P.S. I tried the lipstick bit on my grandmother. You're right. It makes older people look cheerier.

Pick a Pen Pal!

by Randy Harelson

There's a special thrill in writing to a pen pal who lives far away. The customs and holidays and even the climate may be different from your own. There's the surprise of stamps and postmarks you've never seen before. It's interesting to learn about another country from someone your own age. You'll be making a new friend at the same time. All of these things make having a pen pal a lot of fun!

Of course, a pen pal doesn't have to live in a different country. You can have fun and learn more about your own country by writing to someone in a different part of the United States.

Sometimes pen friendships last for years. The pals may even visit as well as write letters.

How can you find a pen pal? Follow these directions carefully:

1. Write a letter to a pen pal group such as:

   International Friendship League, Inc.
   55 Mount Vernon Street
   Boston, Massachusetts 02108
   Ages 7–60

   Include your full name, address, age, date of birth, sex, and hobbies or interests. If you can read or write another language, say so.

2. Ask for a pen pal form.

3. Include a self-addressed stamped envelope.

Once you get your pen pal's name and address, copy it down and put it in a safe place. A lost name or address cannot be replaced. Write to your new pen pal as soon as possible. Be sure to include your full name and address on both the letter and the envelope.

For overseas pen pals, you may want to use an aerogramme. An aerogramme is writing paper, envelope, and postage all-in-one. You can get aerogrammes at any post office. Remember that a letter from the United States to Canada or Mexico costs the same as a letter to any state in the United States. A letter to any country outside North America costs more and should be weighed and stamped with airmail stamps at your post office.

Finally, write neatly and clearly— English may be a new language to your pen pal!

Think About It

1. What made Joseph change his mind about having a pen pal?
2. How did Joseph's and Aunt Helen's letters show that they were becoming friends?
3. Why did having a pen pal help both Joseph and Aunt Helen?
4. Would you like to have a pen pal? Tell why or why not.
5. What does "Pick a Pen Pal!" say that you can do if you want to have a pen pal?

Explore   See how many reasons you can list to explain why people write letters. Check with family members about why they write letters and what types of letters they receive in the mail.

Create and Share   Add to a class bulletin board about letter writing your list of reasons for writing letters. Pick one of the reasons for letter writing and create or bring in from home an example of that type of letter.

A Grain of Wheat
A WRITER BEGINS

by Clyde Robert Bulla

One year when I was very young, I got three books for Christmas. Those books were read to me until I knew them by heart. From the ABC book I learned the letters—"A is an apple pie, B bit it, C cut it," and all the rest. From *Mother Goose* I learned about verses and rhymes. And *Peter Rabbit* was a good story with good pictures. I held the books in front of me and pretended to read. I made pencil marks in a tablet and pretended I was writing.

My mother taught me to write *Clyde*.

"Now when you go to school, you'll know how to write your name," she said.

I wanted to read and write, but I didn't want to go to school. Someone had told me tales of what went on at school. They must have frightened me.

Those were the days of country schools. Ours was the Bray School. My sister Louise had taught there before she was married. My sister Corrine had just finished high school and was ready to take Louise's place.

Corrine was teaching for the first time. I was going to school for the first time.

The schoolhouse was white with a red-brick chimney. It had only one room. The blackboard was up front, along with the teacher's desk and the library. The library was a tall green cupboard with a door.

There were rows of seats and desks for the boys and girls. In the back of the room was a big iron stove.

Corrine and I were the first ones there. She wrote *Welcome* on the blackboard. Boys and girls began to come from the farms in the neighborhood. There were nine boys and nine girls. Two or three rode horses to school, but most of them walked.

I was in the first grade with three other boys—Leonard, Lawrence, and Harold. Later Lawrence and Harold moved away, but Leonard and I were in school together for years.

When we were called up for our first class, we sat on a long bench in front of the teacher's desk. The teacher asked a question. What would we buy if we had a hundred dollars? I've forgotten what Lawrence and Harold answered. Leonard said he would buy a horse. That was a good answer for a farm boy. I said I would buy a table.

The older boys and girls had been listening. They all laughed at my answer.

Corrine said, "Why would you buy a *table?*"

I said I didn't know.

On the playground, the girls and boys said, "A table—a table! What are you going to do with a table?"

And I knew I must guard against saying stupid things.

Still, I liked school. In first grade we had spelling, numbers, reading, and writing. I was slow at numbers, better at spelling. What I really liked were reading and writing. I wanted to learn new words. I wanted to write them and put them together to see what I could make them say.

I would write *apple.* It could be "*an* apple" or "*the* apple." It could be on a tree or in a dish. It could be green, red, or yellow.

Words were wonderful. By writing them and putting them together, I could make them say whatever I wanted them to say. It was a kind of magic.

Reading was a kind of magic, too. In a book I could meet other people and know what they were doing and feeling and thinking. From a book I could learn about life in other places. Or I could learn everyday things like tying a knot or building a birdhouse.

By the time I was ready for the third grade, I had read most of the books in our school library. There weren't many. I wanted more. Except for my three Christmas books, we had no children's books at home. I began reading whatever I could find in the family bookcase.

There was a thick book called *Oliver Twist*. It had words I didn't know, but there were many I *did* know, and I was able to read the story all the way through.

Lee, the soldier who married my sister, went to California. Louise followed him, but for a time she was in Missouri while he was far away by the Pacific Ocean. I wrote a poem about them:

California and Missouri

Hand in hand,
Over the sand,
Down by the sea,
And there sits Lee.
'Tis California.

Go out and romp
In the swamp
And pick some peas.
There sits Louise.
'Tis Missouri.

It was my first poem.

I started to write a story, but it was never finished. I called it "How Planets Were Born." This is the way it began: "One night old Mother Moon had a million babies . . . "

Now I knew why I had said, in the first grade, that I wanted a table. Even then I wanted to be a writer. And didn't writers sit at tables or desks when they wrote?

I wanted to be a writer. I was sure of that.

"I'm going to write books," I said.

My mother said, "Castles in the air."

"What does that mean?" I asked.

"It means you're having daydreams," she said. "You'll dream of doing a lot of different things, but you probably won't do any of them. As you get older, you'll change."

I went from the second grade to the third to the fourth, and I hadn't changed. I still knew what I wanted to be.

I thought about writing and talked about it. I talked too much.

My father told me he was tired of listening to me.

"You can't be a writer," he said. "What do you know about people? What have you ever done? You don't have anything to write about."

When I thought over what he had said, it seemed to me he was right. I stopped writing. But not for long.

The city nearest us was St. Joseph, Missouri. Our newspaper came from there. In the paper I read about a contest for boys and girls—"Write a story of a grain of wheat in five hundred words or less." First prize was a hundred dollars. There were five second prizes of twenty dollars each. After that there were one hundred prizes of one dollar each.

I began to write my story. It went something like this: "I am a grain of wheat. I grew in a field where the sun shone and the rain fell."

I didn't tell anyone what I was doing. When my story was finished, I made a neat copy. I mailed it in our mailbox down the road.

Time went by. I began to look for the newspaper that would tell who had won the contest. At last it came.

There was a whole page about the contest. I saw I hadn't won the first prize. I hadn't won a second prize either. That was a disappointment. I had thought I might win one of the second prizes.

I read down the long list at the bottom of the page—the names and addresses of the boys and girls who had won the one-dollar prizes. Surely my name would be there. It *had* to be!

I read more and more slowly. Only a few names were left.

And one of them was mine! "Clyde Bulla, King City, Missouri."

"I won!" I shouted.

My mother looked at my name. "That's nice," she said.

Nice? Was that all she could say?

I started to show the paper to my father. There was something in his face that stopped me. I could see he wasn't happy that I had won a prize.

My sister Corrine was there. I could see she wasn't happy either. She was sorry for me because all I had won was a dollar.

Didn't they know it wasn't the dollar that mattered?

I had written a story that was all mine. No one had helped me. I had sent it off by myself. How many other boys and girls had sent their stories? Maybe a thousand or more. But my story had won a prize, and my name was here in the paper. I was a writer. No matter what anyone else might say, I was a writer.

Think About It

1. Why did Clyde think that words were a "kind of magic"?
2. How did Clyde's family feel about his wanting to be a writer? How do you know?
3. How did Clyde make his dream of becoming a writer come true?
4. What does it take to become a writer?

Create and Share   Do a class survey to list favorite authors. Make a chart with the title "Our Favorite Writers." Beside each author's name, list his or her story. Then tell why you chose the author you did.

Explore   Search for more biographical information on the author you chose. A good place to start your search might be on the back jacket flap of a book by that author.

My Friend, My Enemy

by Clyde Robert Bulla

In the story A Grain of Wheat—A Writer Begins, *the author Clyde Robert Bulla tells about his life. From the time he was a young boy, he knew he wanted to be a writer. His first story, as you remember, won a prize.*

Mr. Bulla has been writing ever since. He has written many wonderful stories for young readers. My Friend, My Enemy, *the story you are about to read, is one of them.*

Eric was quiet when he came home from school.

His father asked, "Is anything wrong?"

His mother asked, "Is it Craig again?"

"Yes, it is," said Eric, "and today was the worst yet."

He and Craig were in the third grade at Hilltop School. Craig was the new boy. He had just moved to the farm across the road from Eric.

"We started out being friends. I tried to help him with things," said Eric, "but he never did thank me."

"It's hard for some people to say thank you," said his father.

"What happened today?" asked his mother.

"Freddie Abbott picked a cookie up off the ground and was going to eat it," said Eric. "I told him not to because it had been in the dirt. He started to eat it anyway, and I took it away from him. He raised a big fuss, and Craig came up and said he saw me take the cookie away from Freddie. I tried to tell him why, but he wouldn't listen. He was pushing me, and the teacher came out."

"Did you tell her what happened?" asked his mother.

"Yes, and she said I was right. But Craig never said he was sorry. He just walked away."

"It's hard for some people to say they are sorry," said Eric's father. "Sometimes it takes them a while to learn."

"I don't think Craig will ever learn," said Eric.

The next day Craig came to school on his little black pony. No one else in school had a pony. He was a good rider, and all the others watched him ride up and down.

"Who wants a free ride on Jip?" he asked.

"I do," said three or four boys and girls.

They stood in line to ride with Craig. One after another they got up behind him, and Jip took them across the playground and back.

Eric was sitting on the schoolhouse steps. Craig rode up to him. They looked at each other but didn't speak. After a little while, Craig rode away and tied Jip to the fence.

Jenny Bryant asked Eric, "Why didn't you take a ride?"

"Craig didn't want me to," said Eric.

"Yes, he did," said Jenny. "That's why he rode over to you."

Eric shook his head. "He wanted me to ask so he could say no."

"Why would he do that?" asked Jenny.

"Because we're enemies," said Eric.

"It isn't good to have enemies," said Jenny.

"I know," said Eric, "but sometimes it happens."

"What will you do when you have your birthday party?" she asked. "Will you invite Craig?"

"He wouldn't come if I did," said Eric.

The next Saturday he was out raking the yard. He could look up the road and see Craig's house. He saw Craig and his father and mother drive off in their car.

Across the road was the pasture where Craig kept his pony. The pony was standing by the gate.

"Hello, Jip," called Eric. "Are you lonesome all by yourself?"

He finished with the yard. Then he saw that the gate was open and the pony was out in the road. Eric tried to drive him back into the pasture, but the pony kicked up his heels and ran away.

Eric called to his mother, "Craig's pony is out. If I don't stop him, he might go all the way to Canada!"

He ran down the road and caught up with Jip. He tried to drive him back, and he tried to coax him.

Jip would not be driven or coaxed. He kept tossing his head and dancing away.

Eric went home and got a rope. Again he ran out after Jip. The pony was eating grass by the side of the road.

Eric had tied a noose in the rope. "Here, boy," he said.

The pony looked up. Eric threw the noose. It was a good throw. It sailed over Jip's head and settled around his neck.

"I've got you," said Eric.

Jip danced a little more. Then he gave up and let himself be led back to the pasture. As Eric closed the gate, he saw that Craig and his father and mother had just come home.

He went to the barn and put away the rope.

When he came out, Craig was there. Craig's face was red. He said in an angry voice, "If you wanted to ride my pony, why didn't you say so?"

Eric was too surprised to answer.

"I saw what you did," said Craig. "You waited till I was gone, and then you took him out and rode him."

"I *never* rode him," said Eric.

"I saw you!" Craig was shouting. "I saw you put him back in the pasture."

"He was out in the road," said Eric. "I caught him and brought him back."

"He was in the road because you took him there."

"He got out himself. The gate was open."

"It *wasn't* open. I put him in the pasture, and I shut the gate. I always shut the gate when I . . ."

"Wait a minute," Eric broke in. He was looking across the road. Jip was at the gate. With his nose, he was pushing at the bar that held the gate shut.

Craig turned and looked too. They watched as Jip pushed at the bar until it lifted. The gate swung open. Jip started out into the road.

Craig shouted, "Yo! Jip!"

The pony jumped back and ran off across the pasture.

Craig went over and shut the gate. He didn't look at Eric as he turned toward home.

Eric talked about it later with his mother and father. "The pony found out how to open the gate. Craig saw it himself, and he didn't say he was sorry for what he had said to me. He just went home."

"Maybe he will say something at school," said his mother. But Monday came, and Craig said nothing to Eric.

Eric was inviting boys and girls to his birthday party. He invited everyone in the third grade— everyone but Craig.

And then, on Tuesday, he did invite Craig. He wasn't sure why except that Craig *was* in the third grade and he looked unhappy, as if he felt left out. Eric went up to him and said, "I'm having a birthday party next Saturday at 2 o'clock. Do you want to come?"

And Craig didn't answer.

On Saturday, the boys and girls were at Eric's. They were playing in the big orchard behind the barn.

"Look!" said someone. "There's Craig!"

"I thought he wasn't coming," said someone else.

But there was Craig, riding up on Jip. He jumped off. He tossed the reins over the pony's head and put them in Eric's hands.

"Here," he said. "I brought Jip—for your party. You can have pony rides. I'll come and get him afterward."

He walked away.

"Wait," said Eric.

The others took it up. "Wait, Craig. Come back."

They ran after him. "Don't go. We need you to ride the pony," they said until he stopped.

"Well—all right," he said.

Back in the orchard, the boys and girls lined up for their rides.

"Eric first," said Craig, "because it's his birthday."

So Eric had the first ride around the orchard. The others took their turns. After that, they played games. Then Eric's mother brought out a big cake and homemade ice cream. The time went by so fast, it seemed the party was over before it began.

Eric said to Craig, "Thank you for the pony rides."

Craig grinned. "You won't have to chase Jip down the road anymore. I wired the gate shut."

That evening Eric and his mother and father talked about the party.

"Everybody seemed to have a good time," said his mother.

"I'm glad Craig came. Now we're not enemies," said Eric. "But do you know something? He never said he was sorry, and he never thanked me for bringing his pony back."

"I think he did thank you," said his mother.

"I think he said he was sorry too," said his father. "People have different ways of saying thank you and I'm sorry."

Think About It.

1. What is there about Eric that makes you think of Clyde Robert Bulla as a young boy?
2. Why doesn't Clyde Robert Bulla write about a boy who lives in the city?
3. What kind of person was Craig?
4. Tell how and why Eric's feelings about Craig changed during the story.
5. Do you think Eric and Craig will be friends? Why or why not?

Create and Share Work with a partner to make a list of things that could go in a class writing corner. Think of different things to write with and different things to write on. Share your list.

Explore Find and read another story by Clyde Robert Bulla. This author has written many interesting stories for and about young people.

My Diary

by Bernard Waber

This is my diary. It's very private... and very personal. I won't let anyone read it.

Not even your mother? Not even your father?

Not even my mother. Not even my father.

May I look at it?

NO! It's personal and private.

May I just peek at the color of the pages? Well...

Please? Oh please?

All right... just the color of the pages.

There! Pink! Oh, how beautiful!

May I just peek at the first word on the first page?

NO!

Dear Diary.

by Jan Hurwitz

July 7, 9:00 P.M.

Dear Diary,

Remember yesterday I was bored because my friends were all away on vacation this summer? Well, I'm not bored anymore! I'm scared!

Mom said I could leave my bedroom light on all night. I know I won't sleep at all. I've got my baseball bat, hockey stick, and a pile of rocks in bed with me. My drum is here too. Maybe noise will scare them away. Hope it's enough protection—oh, oh, I can hear the sound of their feet coming closer and closer. More later . . .

July 8, 9:00 P.M.

Hi Diary,

I scared them away by banging the walls and the closet door with my baseball bat. Mom clanged a pot cover on a pot. Dad blew his trumpet real loud right into the closet keyhole. We looked and sounded so silly I got the giggles. I was so tired I fell asleep and forgot to finish telling you what happened.

It started yesterday morning in the kitchen. We heard tiny feet, lots and lots of tiny feet, running inside the ceiling. Then we heard the sound of sharp teeth chewing through wood and plaster, like lots of little saws.

Dad ran outside to look at the back of our house. He called Mom and me to see what had invaded our home. I couldn't believe what I saw.

Big holes were chewed out of the wood. One hole was an entrance door and another an escape exit, Dad said. Around the side of the house were three more big holes. Our house looked like a piece of swiss cheese with holes all over it.

Beady little black eyes looked down at us from inside the holes. They were squirrels, with ratty gray fur and sharp teeth. Yuck! There were three of them, one big one and two smaller ones. They sat in the holes scolding us for bothering them.

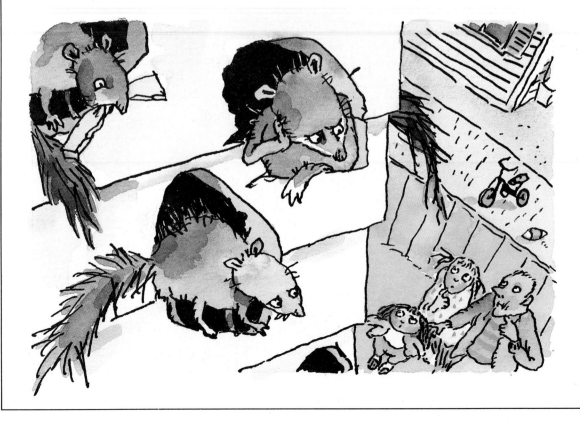

Mom ran to the telephone to tell Gramps all about it. He said he'd be right over with a trap.

The trap Gramps brought was a big steel trap. It caught, but didn't hurt, small animals. We smushed peanut butter on a tray inside the trap. Squirrels love peanut butter. It's my favorite food too.

Either the squirrels weren't hungry, or they were too smart to go near the trap. Mom and Dad were very disappointed. Me too!

So tonight I'll sleep in Mom and Dad's bedroom. They'll protect me. More news tomorrow.

July 9, 12:00 Noon

Hi Diary,

Wow! What a day!! I couldn't wait to tell you about it.

We forgot to close the trap overnight. A skunk smelled the peanut butter and went into the trap. It's a big grown-up skunk. I can't believe it. I didn't even know there were skunks around here.

Dad just shook his head when he saw it, told Mom to take care of it, and went off to work. Mom yelled, "Thanks a lot, Mike!" to him. She wasn't very happy about being left alone to take care of a skunk. Dad just laughed.

The skunk is really a pretty animal and very gentle-looking. It has soft, trusting eyes and seems friendly. The trap is small, so the skunk can't raise its tail to spray us with skunk perfume. Lucky us!

Mom says skunks are nocturnal. That means skunks sleep all day and are awake all night. She tied a long rope to the trap's door handle then carried the rope as far away from the trap as she could.

We went to the store and rented another trap. Then we carefully filled the feeding bin with lots of crunchy peanut butter and put peanuts on top of it. Yum! I'll have some of that for *my* lunch.

It worked! We caught the biggest-size squirrel. It ran back and forth in the cage, trying to escape. Mom and I laughed and clapped our hands. We were so happy.

Now we're waiting for Dad to come home. He'll help us set the skunk free. Then we'll take the trapped squirrel for a ride in our car.

Gramps said we have to drive ten miles away so it can't find its way back to our house.

I'll write more tonight.

July 9, 8:00 P.M.

Here I am again. We let the squirrel loose in the woods. While we were driving in the car, it hissed and growled at us. When we opened the trap door, it ran out fast and climbed the nearest tree.

Back home, at sunset, Mom pulled the rope opening the cage door to let the skunk out. The skunk waddled away slowly and went home, I guess.

Grandma and Grandpa brought us five boxes of moth balls because squirrels hate the smell of moth balls. Me too!

Gramps and Dad climbed up ladders to toss the moth balls into all of the chewed holes. Then we watched to see what would happen.

Two squirrels jumped out of their holes and onto our roof. They rubbed their eyes and noses real hard with their paws and were crying. Then they ran away. Hurray! We won!

I'm glad it's all over. We celebrated our victory with delicious banana splits—yum!

July 10, 9:00 P.M.

Dear Diary,

Nothing much to write about. What a boring day. Wish my friends were back from vacation. I'm, bored, bored, BORED——

July 11, 10 A.M.

Dear Diary,

Did I say I was bored? Mom's screams from the cellar woke me up early this morning.

Dad was shaving, and he went running down to the cellar with white glop all over his face yelling, "Laura, are you OK? What's the matter?"

I ran downstairs to go into the cellar too.

Dad yelled to me from the cellar, "Tina, don't come down here! Stay upstairs!"

"What's going on, Dad? Mom, what's wrong? Are you OK?" I yelled louder than they were yelling so they could hear me.

"It's a skunk, Tina. It dug a tunnel through the dirt under our porch and found a way to get into the cellar. Mom was putting dirty clothes into the washing machine when she saw it sleeping on a soft pile of towels that the skunk had pushed together to make a nest. When Mom screamed, it got frightened and ran outside."

I sat down on the top cellar step. Was it the same skunk as the one in our trap? Did it decide it liked me? Did it move into our cellar to live near me?

Wow! Did I say I was bored?

Wonder what the skunk will do next? Maybe it has some babies it will bring to show me. What a great exciting summer this has turned out to be!

I'm glad I wrote all of this down as it happened, in my very own diary.

Gramps says, "A thought written down is yours to enjoy forever . . . "

Think About It

1. What do people write about in a diary?
2. What lesson did the writer of the diary learn in "My Diary"?
3. Did you find "Dear Diary" interesting to read? Why or why not?
4. In THAT'S WRITE! you have read a lot about why people write. What is your favorite reason and way to write?

Create and Share   Put pieces of notebook paper together to make your own diary. Write in it for one week. Tell the class what you like about your diary but do not tell what you have written. Your diary is private!

Explore   Bernard Waber has written many funny books. Read another book by him.

Abra-cadabra !

Abracadabra
Nothing up my sleeve
A little hocus-pocus
Now what will I retrieve?

The Garden of Abdul Gasazi

by Chris Van Allsburg

Six times Miss Hester's dog Fritz had bitten dear cousin Eunice. So when Miss Hester received an invitation to visit Eunice she was not surprised to read "P.S., Please leave your dog home." On the day of her visit Miss Hester asked young Alan Mitz to stay with Fritz and give him his afternoon walk.

As soon as Miss Hester left, Fritz ran into the parlor. He loved to chew on the chairs and shake the stuffing out of the pillows. But Alan was ready. All morning long he kept Fritz from sinking his sharp little teeth into the furniture. Finally the dog gave up and fell asleep exhausted. Alan took a nap, too, but first he hid his hat under his shirt, hats being one of Fritz's favorite things to chew.

An hour later Alan quickly awoke when Fritz gave him a bite on the nose. The bad-mannered dog was ready for his afternoon walk. Alan fastened Fritz's leash and the dog dragged him out of the house. Walking along, they discovered a small white bridge at the side of the road. Alan decided to let Fritz lead the way across.

177

Some distance beyond the bridge Alan stopped to read a sign. It said: ABSOLUTELY, POSITIVELY NO DOGS ALLOWED IN THIS GARDEN. At the bottom it was signed: ABDUL GASAZI, RETIRED MAGICIAN. Behind the sign stood a vine-covered wall with an open doorway. Alan took the warning quite seriously. He turned to leave, but as he did, Fritz gave a tremendous tug and snapped right out of his collar. He bolted straight ahead through the open door, with Alan running right behind.

"Fritz, stop, you bad dog!" cried Alan, but the dog simply ignored him. Down shadowed paths and across sunlit lawns they raced, deeper and deeper into the garden. Finally, Alan drew close enough to grab hold of Fritz. But as he reached out he slipped and fell. Fritz barked with laughter as he galloped out of sight. Alan slowly picked himself up. He knew he had to find Fritz before Mr. Gasazi discovered him. Bruised and tired, he hurried off in the dog's direction.

After a long search Alan was ready to give up. He was afraid he might never find Fritz. But then he came upon fresh dog prints. Slowly he followed Fritz's tracks along a path that led into a forest. The dirt path ended and a brick wall began. There were no more tracks to follow, but Alan was certain that Fritz must be just ahead.

178

Alan started running. In front of him he could see a clearing in the forest. As he came dashing out of the woods he stopped as quickly as if he had run up against a wall. For there, in front of him, stood a truly awesome sight. It was the house of Gasazi. Alan nervously climbed the great stairs convinced Fritz had come this way and been captured.

The boy's heart was pounding when he arrived at the huge door. He took a deep breath and reached for the bell, but before he touched it the door swung open. There, in the shadow of the hallway, stood Gasazi the Great. "Greetings, do come in" was all that he said.

Alan followed Gasazi into a large room. When the magician turned around Alan quickly apologized for letting Fritz into the garden. He politely asked that, if Mr. Gasazi had Fritz, would he please give him back? The magician listened carefully and then, smiling, said, "Certainly you may have your little Fritzie. Follow me." With those words he went to the door and led Alan back outside.

They were walking across the lawn when suddenly Gasazi stopped by a gathering of ducks. He began to speak in a voice that was more like a growl. "I detest dogs. They dig up my flowers, they chew on my trees. Do you know what I do to dogs I find in my garden?" "What?" whispered Alan, almost afraid to hear the answer. "I TURN THEM INTO DUCKS!" yelled Gasazi. In horror, Alan looked at the birds in front of him. When one duck came forward, Gasazi said, "There's your Fritz." Alan begged the magician to change Fritz back. "Impossible," he answered, "only time can do that. This spell may last years or perhaps just a day. Now take your dear bird and please don't come again."

When Alan took the bird in his arms it tried to give him a bite. "Good old boy," said Alan sadly as he patted the bird on the head. "You really haven't changed so much." With tears in his eyes he started for home. Behind him Alan could hear Gasazi laughing. As he approached the stairway, a gust of wind took Alan's hat sailing right off his head. Running along with one arm reaching for the hat, Alan lost his hold on Fritz. The duck flew out ahead and grabbed the hat in midair. But instead of landing he just kept on flying, higher and higher, until he disappeared in the afternoon clouds.

Alan just stood and stared at the empty sky. "Good-bye, old fellow," he called out sadly, sure that Fritz was gone forever. At least he had something to chew on. Slowly, one step after

another, Alan found his way back to the garden gate and over the bridge. It was sunset by the time he reached Miss Hester's. Lights were on and he knew she must be home. With a heavy heart he approached the door, wondering how Miss Hester would take the news.

When Miss Hester came to the door, Alan blurted out his incredible story. He could barely hold back the tears; then, racing out of the kitchen, dog food on his nose, came Fritz. Alan couldn't believe his eyes. "I'm afraid Mr. Gasazi played a trick on you," said Miss Hester, trying to hide a smile. "Fritz was in the front yard when I returned. He must have found his own way home while you were with Mr. Gasazi. You see, Alan, no one can really turn dogs into ducks; that old magician just made you think that duck was Fritz."

Alan felt very silly. He promised himself he'd never be fooled like that again. He was too old to believe in magic. Miss Hester watched from the porch as Alan waved goodbye and hurried down the road to go home. Then she called out to Fritz, who was playfully running around the front yard. He came trotting up the front steps with something in his mouth and dropped it at Miss Hester's feet. "Why you bad dog," she said. "What are you doing with Alan's hat?"

Think About It

1. Dog-sitting with Fritz was not an easy job for Alan! Why?
2. Do you believe Mr. Gasazi turned Fritz into a duck? Why or why not?
3. Why was the ending of this story a surprise?
4. What will Alan think when Miss Hester returns his hat?

Create and Share
The author doesn't really tell you or show you what happened when Fritz was lost. It is left up to you to decide. If you think the Great Gasazi did turn Fritz into a duck, illustrate his doing that. If you think he did not change Fritz into a duck, illustrate what happened to Fritz.

Explore
Chris Van Allsburg has written and illustrated many other books for children. Look for another one of his books to enjoy and share.

ISHKABIBBLE!

A Take-Your-Pick Adventure

by Hal Ober

Introduction

In this story there is magic, and **you** *make it happen. Every adventure in the story happens to* **you**. *Also, there are many different adventures to choose from, and* **you** *decide how to get to them.*

Just begin reading on the next page. Soon you will have to make a choice about what happens next. Turn to the page you've chosen and read on. Keep reading—and choosing— until the story tells you it's THE END. *Then go back to the beginning and pick a new trail to a new ending.*

Get ready . . . there's magic ahead!

It's your birthday! All your friends are here at your party. You've had cake and ice cream, and now it's time for a special treat. The Amazing Mayzie, a famous magician, is going to perform for you and your friends in your living room.

Here she is now, in a long red cape and red top hat.

"I would like a volunteer," she says. Many hands shoot up, but she picks you!

"Now—for my first trick," she says, "I will pull a rabbit out of my hat." She hands you her tall red hat and tells you to hold it steady. "And no peeking inside!" Then she closes her eyes and starts to mumble magic words.

Meanwhile your curiosity is growing. Wouldn't it be fun to try on the hat—or at least to feel what's inside?

If you try on the hat, turn to page 190.

If you reach inside the hat, turn to page 195.

189

You try on the hat. Instantly there is a clap of thunder and a flash of light. Something like an earthquake knocks you off your feet. When you come to, you are no longer in your living room. You are in a palace, standing in the middle of a great throne room.

There is a sound of trumpets. "The royal wizard!" call the guards. One of them shoves you forward. (Who, *me?* you think.)

A grumpy-looking king is sitting on the throne. "Yo, Wizard," he growls. "Cast me a spell and make it good. Or else!"

A spell? Quickly you say the first magic word that comes to mind: "Ishkabibble!"

The throne room starts to fill up with a purple fog. Now's your chance to escape! Or you can wait and see if you really did cast a spell.

If you escape, turn to page 199.

If you wait and see, turn to page 196.

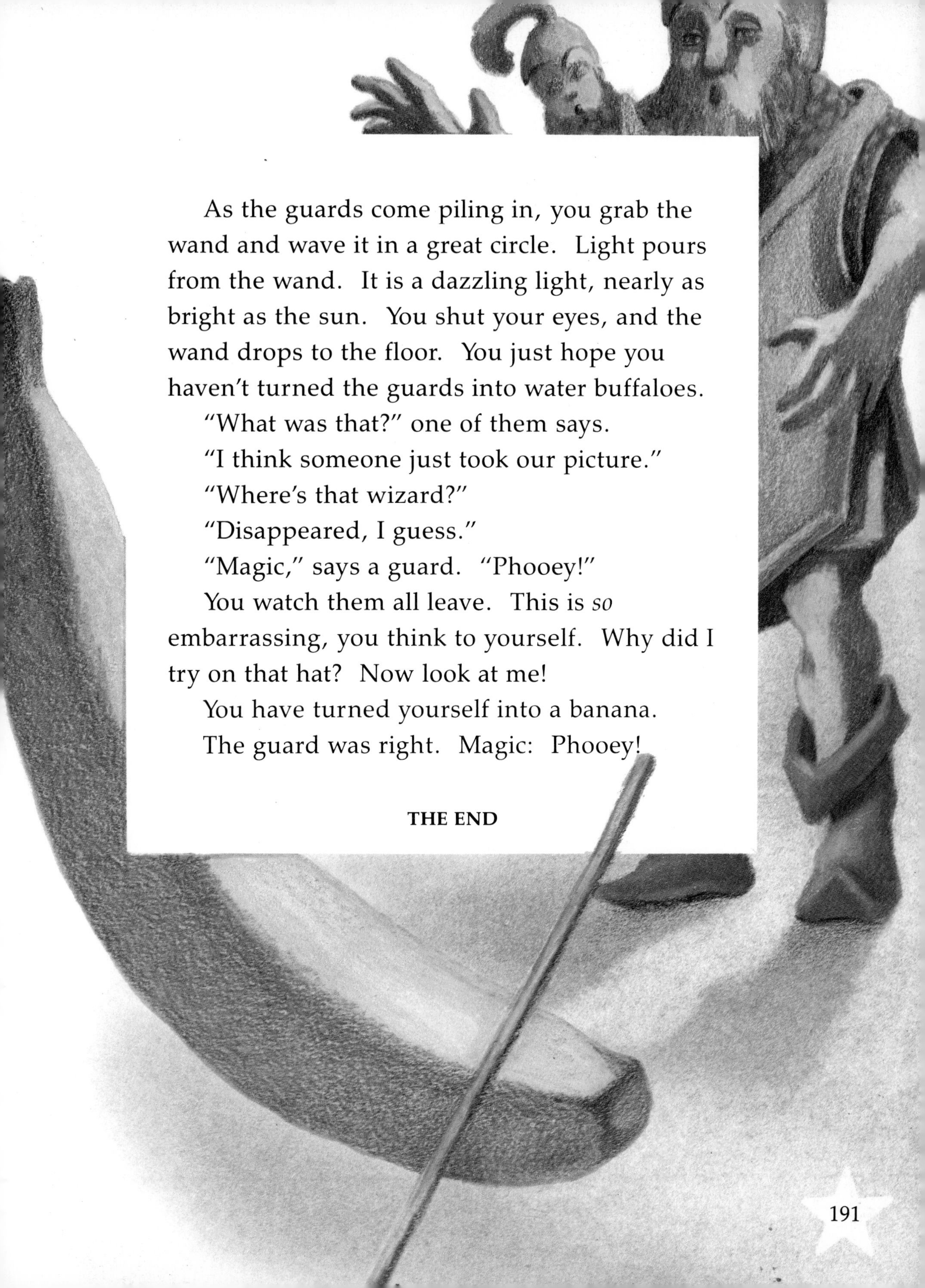

As the guards come piling in, you grab the wand and wave it in a great circle. Light pours from the wand. It is a dazzling light, nearly as bright as the sun. You shut your eyes, and the wand drops to the floor. You just hope you haven't turned the guards into water buffaloes.

"What was that?" one of them says.

"I think someone just took our picture."

"Where's that wizard?"

"Disappeared, I guess."

"Magic," says a guard. "Phooey!"

You watch them all leave. This is *so* embarrassing, you think to yourself. Why did I try on that hat? Now look at me!

You have turned yourself into a banana.

The guard was right. Magic: Phooey!

THE END

"Going up," says Robert.

The magician is holding him by the back of his neck. You're hanging on to his hind legs. This is one heavy rabbit. You can hear the magician grunting and gasping, not knowing that she is pulling you up too. And then—OOF! Out you both come! CRASH! The magician falls backward, tipping over the table lamp, and the room goes dark.

When the lights come on again, the magician is nowhere to be seen. Instead, Robert is sitting there, waiting for the noise to die down.

"Get me out of here!" calls a muffled voice.

"For my first trick," says Robert, "I will do something I have always wanted to do. I will pull a magician out of a hat!"

THE END

192

"Give it your best shot," you tell the wizard. The old man lifts his arms above his head. "Presto-Zesto!" he cries.

Right away all the straw in the dungeon starts whirling around. Pretty soon you're flying around too. After a while, the tornado stops and you land on something hard. When you dare to open your eyes, you see that you and the wizard are sitting in your schoolroom!

"You're both late," says the teacher. "Get busy and wash the chalkboards."

"Sorry about this," mutters the wizard. Then he looks at you closely. "Hey, wait a minute," he says. "That's *Mayzie's* hat! You're a fake!"

"Oops!" you say. "I just remembered I'm late for a birthday party!" and you dash out the door.

THE END

You take a deep breath. "Ishkabibble!" you yell.

"That's a new one," says the wizard.

Where is the floor? Everything around you is starting to disappear! You feel as if you're flying. Clouds whiz past you. "Caw!" A crow almost flies into you. You hold onto your hat with all your might.

What's that rumbling sound down below? It's getting louder. Suddenly—ker-plunk!—you and the wizard drop through the clouds into the seats of a roaring roller coaster.

"Wow!" shouts the wizard as you go whipping around a corner, "That's some magic!"

"It was nothing!" you yell back.

"By the way," he shouts, "Happy Birthday!"

THE END

You peek into the hat. A soft furry paw shakes your hand. You have to take a closer look. Peering deep into the hat, you see a white rabbit sitting in front of a TV set. "Hi, there!" calls the rabbit. "My name's Robert! Come on down!"

"I'd like to, but I'm too big," you call back.

"No problem! Just say, Ishkabibble!"

"*Ishkabibble?*"

Suddenly the hat starts growing—or else you're shrinking. You trip over the hat brim and land in Robert's easy chair. "Welcome!" he says.

Just then the magician's hand reaches down into the hat. "No privacy," Robert sighs.

"Why don't I come up with you?" you grin.

"I have a better idea," says Robert. He pulls back a rug and opens a trap door. "This way!"

If you come up with Robert, turn to page 192.

If you go down with Robert, turn to page 198.

You wait. The fog clears, and you see the king has turned into a kangaroo. He is not amused. In fact, he is hopping mad.

"Sorry, Your Majesty," you say, trying not to giggle.

"Arrest this scoundrel!" the king roars.

The guards march you down to the dungeon. As the doors clang shut, you discover another prisoner—lying in midair!

"Hello," he says, tipping his pointy hat. "You must be the new wizard. I'm the old wizard. The king threw me in here this morning after I turned him into a penguin. But don't worry. Now that I've had my nap, we can escape. I have a magic word."

"So do I," you say. "My word will get us out of here, *easily*. At least, I think it will."

If you try your magic word, turn to page 194.

If you try the wizard's, turn to page 193.

196

You have never played a flute before. But as the guards rush in, you begin to play a beautiful tune! All at once they start marching around the room, around and around, until suddenly you stop.

Quickly they scramble to sit down on a trunk or box, just like in a game of Musical Chairs.

"I was here first!" says a guard.

"No way! I was!" says another voice. You turn around. It's Mayzie the Magician! The palace and the guards are gone. You are back at your birthday party, playing a *real* game of musical chairs.

"So there!" says Mayzie, sticking out her tongue.

"Okay! we'll do it over," you say, and you start up the record of flute music again.

"What a cry baby," you think to yourself. "I'd better give her back her *hat!*"

THE END

Carefully you follow Robert down a rickety ladder into a small garage. "Here's my pride and joy," he says, pointing to his shiny black Bunnymobile 5000. "Hop in! We'll go for a ride."

Soon you are riding through a storybook land of rolling hills and puffy clouds. Mice on bicycles pass with a wave. Crocodiles in jogging suits run by.

"Uh—oh," says Robert. "We're being followed."

In the rearview mirror, you can see a red motorcycle coming up fast. It's Mayzie the Magician!

"We'll lose her in the Enchanted Forest," says Robert. But the motorcycle keeps up with every twist and turn. Then up ahead the road divides. One sign points to Ishkabibble, the other to Oshkabobble. Which road should you take?

If you take Ishkabibble, turn to page 200.

If you take Oshkabobble, turn to page 203.

198

Out of the throne room you run, slipping on the marble floor and skidding down the long hallway.

"Blast this fog!" you hear the king sputter. "After the rascal!"

You glance over your shoulder. A hundred royal guards are hot on your heels.

"Ishkabibble!" you yell at them, but this time nothing happens.

You run up a flight of stairs, through the royal kitchen where you knock over a big pot of pea soup. Next you run down another hallway. It ends in a dead end.

There are two doors at the end of the hall. One door is red, the other blue.

That slippery soup won't stop the guards for long. Here they come now, angrier than ever. Pick a door, fast!

If you pick the red door, turn to page 201.

If you pick the blue door, turn to page 202.

199

Darkness swallows you up like a whale. Bats wearing sunglasses fly past the headlights, singing "Beep!" You are inside Ishkabibble Mountain. The tunnel gets bumpier. Then it stops.

Robert hops out of the car. "So long," he says. "I'm supposed to meet Alice in Wonderland, and I'm late!"

"I don't want to be stuck here!" you yell. "It's dark, and I can't see my hand in front of my . . . "

POP!

It wasn't a mountain you were stuck in. It was the magician's hat. And now you're free.

"Didn't I tell you not to peek inside?" says the magician in her sternest voice. "Magic can be tricky."

"Time to unwrap your presents!" your mom says.

"Thanks for unwrapping *me*," you tell the Amazing Mayzie.

THE END

You open the red door and rush in and lock the door behind you. It's pitch dark. You grope around. All you feel are clothes on hangers. You're in a coat closet! You hear the guards trying to break the door down. Quickly you run to the back of the closet. You grab what feels like a cape off a hanger and wrap it around you. Maybe they won't find you. Just then you hear the door burst open, and the guards rush in.

"You try over there; we'll try over here!" they shout.

Coats are sliding and squeaking. The guards are grumbling. But suddenly they start laughing. What's so funny? You take a peek and—hey! Those aren't the guards. They're all your *friends.* You're back home at your party. Now you're wearing the magician's cape *and* hat, and she doesn't look too pleased.

THE END

You open the blue door. There is another stairway going up. Up you run, around and around. You can hear the guards' boots echoing on the stairs below you. Finally you reach the tower door at the top of the stairs. Panting, you stumble into a kind of attic, full of old crates and boxes.

You spot a heavy trunk and push it against the door. There is a label on the trunk: PROPERTY OF ROYAL WIZARD. The lid of the trunk is open. A strange light seems to be coming from it. You lift the lid. Inside, on a pile of dusty books, are a silver wand and a golden flute. Both are glowing with a magical light. Suddenly the trunk shakes. The guards are about to force the door open. If you ever needed magic, you need it now! But which should you use—the magic wand or the magic flute?

If you use the magic wand, turn to page 191.

If you play the magic flute, turn to page 197.

"Well, here we are," says Robert. "The Oshkabobble Desert. This is as far as I go."

"What do you mean?" you ask.

"My batteries are running out. See, I'm not a real rabbit. I'm kind of a robot rabbit."

"Robert . . . the Robot Rabbit?" you say.

"I see you found the rabbit in my hat," says Mayzie the Magician.

You blink and look around. You're back at the birthday party! And in your hand is a white stuffed rabbit.

"Sorry," you say. "I guess I got curious."

"Good! Imagination is the best magic of all. Keep the bunny as a birthday present. Just be sure to feed him lots of these!" And she pulls a bunch of carrots from behind your ear.

THE END

Hocus Pocus: Magic You Can Do

*from the book by Ray Broekel
and Laurence B. White, Jr.*

You can learn how to do magic tricks, but that won't make you a magician. Good magicians keep their audiences fooled and entertained by using a number of tools.

Patter is what a magician says. Imagine two different magicians who do the same trick. The first magician explains the trick and says ABRACADABRA. The second magician explains the trick in a very funny way and says GOOEY, GOOEY, SOFT AND CHEWY. Which of these magicians would you rather watch? The first one is just doing a trick. The second is an entertainer.

Timing is another important magician's tool. Timing means doing or saying exactly the right thing at exactly the right time.

Sleight of hand is a magician's term for a secret action. These tricks depend on a magician's skill with his or her hands. One common sleight is a *palm*—keeping an object hidden in your hand.

Gimmicks are special pieces of equipment that make a trick work but are unknown to the audience. In one trick the gimmick might be a magnet. Gimmicks must be your greatest secret.

Misdirection is the magician's most important tool. Suppose you are palming a paper ball in your right hand and don't want your audience to look closely at that hand. You hold your right hand still and point with your left hand to some balls on the table. People will look at the balls on the table. That's misdirection. It takes a suprising amount of practice.

Practice is what sets a magician apart from people who just "do a trick or two." Sometimes it helps to practice the different parts of a trick separately, before putting them all together to do the whole trick. Practice alone, in front of a mirror or in front of friends. Only after lots of practice can you hope to be a real magician.

The Invisible Machine

Ask a friend to clasp his or her hands together and squeeze tightly. The squeezing is important.

As your friend holds his or her hands in that position, you reach into your pocket and pretend to bring something out. "This," you explain (showing nothing), "is my invisible machine. You'll notice that it has a screw on each side." You point to two places about four inches apart. Of course, there is nothing to see.

"Let me show you how my machine works," you say. "Keep your hands clasped together but stick out your two pointing fingers and hold them about an inch apart."

When your friend has done this, you pretend to place the invisible machine on top of his or her fingers. Be careful not to touch the fingers yourself.

"Now watch what happens when I tighten the screw." You put one of your hands on each side of the extended fingers and begin to twist as though you were tightening invisible screws.

Even *you* will be amazed to see the extended fingers slowly and mysteriously move toward each other as if some invisible force were pushing them together.

Think About It

1. What does it take to be a good magician?
2. Why is it important to do each part of a magic trick in the right order?
3. Why do people think these tricks are magic?
4. Do you think it is fun to do magic tricks? Why or why not?
5. What is the same about all magic tricks?

Explore   Look under *magic* in the library card catalog. Find a magic trick that you would like to practice or be able to do.

Create and Share   Tell the class about the magic trick you found. Describe how it is done and what seems magical about it. If you can, perform the trick for others.

A my name is Andrew,
    My sister's name is Anne.
We live in Akron,
    And we sell apples.

B my name is Bertha,
    My brother's name is Bob.
We live in Biloxi,
    And we sell books.

You Name It!

Tikki Tikki Tembo

retold by Arlene Mosel

Once upon a time, a long, long time ago, it was the custom of all the fathers and mothers in China to give their first and honored sons great long names. But second sons were given hardly any name at all.

In a small mountain village there lived a mother who had two little sons. Her second son she called Chang, which meant "little or nothing." But her first and honored son, she called Tikki tikki tembo-no sa rembo-chari bari ruchi-pip peri pembo, which meant "the most wonderful thing in the whole wide world"!

Every morning the mother went to wash in a little stream near her home. The two boys always went chattering along with her. On the bank was an old well.

"Don't go near the well," warned the mother, "or you will surely fall in."

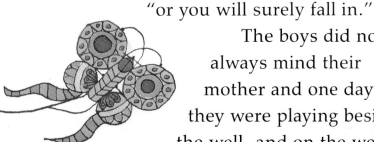

The boys did not always mind their mother and one day they were playing beside the well, and on the well, when Chang fell in!

Tikki tikki tembo-no sa rembo-chari bari ruchi-pip peri pembo ran as fast as his little legs could carry him to his mother and said,

"Most Honorable Mother, Chang has fallen into the well!"

"The water roars, 'Little Blossom,' I cannot hear you," said the mother.

Then Tikki tikki tembo-no sa rembo-chari bari ruchi-pip peri pembo raised his voice and cried,

"Oh, Most Honorable One, Chang has fallen into the well!"

"That troublesome boy," answered the mother. "Run and get the Old Man With The Ladder to fish him out."

Then Tikki tikki tembo-no sa rembo-chari bari ruchi-pip peri pembo ran as fast as his little legs could carry him to the Old Man With The Ladder and said, "Old Man With The Ladder, Chang has fallen into the well. Will you come and fish him out?"

"So," said the Old Man With The Ladder, "Chang has fallen into the well."

He ran as fast as his old legs could carry him. Step over step, step over step he went into the well, picked up little Chang, and step over step, step over step brought him out of the well.

He pumped the water out of him and pushed the air into him, and pumped the water out of him and pushed the air into him, and soon Chang was just as good as ever!

Now for several months the boys did not go near the well. But after the Festival of the Eighth Moon they ran to the well to eat their rice cakes.

They ate near the well, they played around the well, they walked on the well and Tikki tikki tembo-no sa rembo-chari bari ruchi-pip peri pembo fell into the well!

Chang ran as fast as his little legs could carry him to his mother and said, "Oh, Most Honorable Mother, Tikki tikki tembo-no sa rembo-chari bari ruchi-pip peri pembo has fallen into the well!"

"The water roars, 'Little One,' I cannot hear you."

So little Chang took a deep breath.

"Oh, Mother, Most Honorable," he panted, "Tikki tikki tembo-no sa rembo-chari bari ruchi-pip peri pembo has fallen into the well!"

"Tiresome Child, what are you trying to say?" said his mother.

"Honorable Mother!
Chari bari
rembo
tikki tikki,"
he gasped,
"pip pip
has fallen into the well!"

"Son, speak your brother's name with respect."

Poor little Chang was all out of breath from saying that great long name, and he didn't think he could say it one more time. But then he thought of his brother in the old well.

Chang bowed his little head clear to the sand, took a deep breath and slowly, very slowly said,

"Most Honorable Mother, Tikki tikki tembo-no sa rembo-chari bari ruchi-pip peri pembo is at the bottom of the well."

"Oh, not my first and honored son, heir of all I possess! Run quickly and tell the Old Man With The Ladder that your brother has fallen into the well."

So Chang ran as fast as his little legs would carry him to the Old Man With The Ladder. Under a tree the Old Man With The Ladder sat bowed and silent.

"Old Man, Old Man," shouted Chang. "Come right away! Tikki tikki tembo-no sa rembo-chari bari ruchi-pip peri pembo has fallen into the stone well!"

But there was no answer. Puzzled he waited. Then with his very last bit of breath he shouted,

"Old Man With The Ladder, Tikki tikki tembo-no sa rembo-chari bari ruchi-pip peri pembo is at the bottom of the well."

"Miserable child, you disturb my dream. I had floated into a purple mist and found my youth again. There were glittering gateways and jeweled blossoms. If I close my eyes perhaps I will again return."

Poor little Chang was frightened. How could he say that great long name again?

"Please, Old Man With The Ladder, please help my brother out of the cold well."

"So," said the Old Man With The Ladder, "your mother's 'Precious Pearl' has fallen into the well!"

The Old Man With The Ladder hurried as fast as his old legs could carry him. Step over step, step over step he went into the well, and step over step, step over step out of the well with the little boy in his arms. Then he pumped the water out of him and pushed the air into him, and pumped the water out of him and pushed the air into him.

But little Tikki tikki tembo-no sa rembo-chari bari ruchi-pip peri pembo had been in the water so long, all because of his great long name, that the moon rose many times before he was quite the same again.

And from that day to this the Chinese have always thought it wise to give all their children little, short names instead of great long names.

Think About It

1. Why did Tikki tikki tembo's family give him such a long name?
2. What made them sorry they had given him this name?
3. How do you think Tikki tikki tembo felt about his name before he fell in the well? After he fell in the well?
4. What are some good things about having a long name? What are some bad things?
5. How would you feel if you had such a long name?

Explore   Find out as much as you can about your whole name. Why does your family have the last name it does? Why did your parents choose for you the first and middle names they did?

Create and Share   Write your full name on a card in large letters. While holding the card up, share with your class the information you discovered about your name.

Let's Find Out About Names

by Valerie Pitt

Can you imagine what the world would be like if there were no such thing as names?

You might be called by a number instead. You wouldn't be called simply 9 or 11, though, because there are millions of people in the world who have come before you.

You might be number 872,397. Think of the confusion it would cause if you made a telephone call and the operator asked, "Who's calling, please?" Or think how long it would take your teacher to read the class roll.

Thank goodness we do have names. Names are a personal, easy way of telling who people are. Your name is part of you. It is your own private property.

Everyone has at least two names—a first name and a last name. Last names are called surnames. Which is the surname in this name— William Patrick Fowler? Some people have a middle name, too. William Fowler's middle name is Patrick.

Some people have two, three, or four middle names. Prince Charles of England has three middle names. His full name is Charles Philip Arthur George, Prince of Wales.

Surnames, or last names, are family names. You might be part of the Rublowsky family, or the Rosenbaum family, or the Smith family.

Long ago, people did not have surnames. They were known just by their first names. As more and more people were born, things got very confusing. When someone called Alan's name, did he or she mean Alan the father or Alan the son? So in time, Alan's son took on the name of Alanson.

The name Alanson separated the son from the father, but showed they were part of the same family. In the same way, the son of John became Johnson.

How many more last names can you think of, ending in *son*? There are Robinson, Williamson, Michaelson, and many, many more.

Many last names have been handed down for hundreds of years. The first people named Wood may once have lived beside a wood or may have been woodcutters. The first person called Shepard may have been a shepherd in the fields. The first person named Taylor was probably a tailor, sewing and cutting cloth for neighbors.

These names are occupational names because they tell about what someone did for a living— what their occupation was. There are lots of other occupational names still in use, though they do not tell about the person's job today.

Can you think of any? Baker, Farmer, Smith are some examples.

Some last names are descriptive names. Perhaps the first person with the surname of Hardy was a strong person who could hunt and fish for hours without tiring. There are other descriptive names too, like Short and Longfellow.

STRONG APPLE CANNON STAR

BIRD BUSH FISH YOUNG

BERRY KATZ STEED WISE

LAMB SINGER SMILEY WOOD

Because people have to have definite ways of telling one person from another, they have first names as well as surnames. Your parents chose your first name because they liked it and thought it was a good name for you. Some families hand down the same name again and again. If both you and your father are called James, you will add Junior to your name. If your grandfather is living and is also called James, you will be James III—the third James.

Do you know why your parents chose your name? Perhaps it was a family favorite, or maybe you were named after a poem, or a song, or a book, or a flower, or perhaps a nice aunt or uncle.

Most names have definite meanings. The name John is from the Hebrew and means "God is gracious." There are lots of "John"s around the world in many different languages. In France, John is Jean—in Spain, Juan—in Germany, Johannes—in Holland, Jan—in Italy, Giovanni— in Russia, Ivan.

The feminine forms of John are Jane and Jean. These names are loved around the world. The French say Jeanne—the Germans, Johanna—the Italians, Giovanna—the Spanish, Juana. Most of the countries of the world are linked together by names.

Do you know a Vanessa? Vanessa means "butterfly." Irene means "peace." Clare means "bright or clear." Eve means "life." Catherine means "pure." Ann means "grace." Patricia means "noble."

The name Peter comes from the Greek word meaning "rock." Perhaps it was first given to a strong, firm person. William means "strong protector."

What is *your* name? If you want to find out what your name means, go to the library and ask for a book on the meaning of names. You will probably find your name there.

Because your name is yours alone, it comes to mean many things to people who know you. It comes to stand for who you are, what you look like, what you act like. That explains why, if you like someone, you like that person's name too. It stands for the good feelings you have about that person. Maybe you have a friend who loves to read. Perhaps you call him or her Professor or Prof. Professor or Prof is a nickname.

Some people are known by their nicknames more often than by their regular names. Some nicknames are just cruel and silly, but others may tell more about a person than a real name does. Do you have a nickname?

Sometimes friends who want to have a special name for you shorten or change your real name.

A poet wrote a rhyme about the different names a boy was called:

Father calls me William,
Sister calls me Will,
Mother calls me Willie,
But the fellows call me Bill.

Whatever your name is, it stands for something very special. It stands for you.

Think About It

1. What do you think would happen if people had no names?
2. How do you feel when someone forgets your name or doesn't say your name correctly?
3. What nickname would you choose for yourself? Explain why?
4. What did you find out about names in this article?
5. How could you learn more about names?

Explore   Look up the meaning of your first name in a book about names.

Create and Share   Make a colorful drawing of your name. Trace around each letter with different colors. Under your drawing, write your name's meaning and tell where it came from. Hang your artwork up with that of your classmates.

RUMPELSTILTSKIN

retold by Edith H. Tarcov

Once upon a time there was a poor miller who had a beautiful daughter.

One morning, the king came riding by. He stopped to talk to the miller. The miller wanted to say something interesting. So he said: "King, I have a daughter—"

"I suppose she is beautiful," said the king.

"Oh yes. She is beautiful," the miller said. "But she is more than that. My daughter . . . MY daughter . . . can spin straw into gold!"

"Spin straw into gold?" said the king. "Hm. Well! Tell your daughter to come to me this evening."

That evening the miller's daughter came to the king. The king took her into a little room. There was nothing in the room but a heap of straw, a chair, and a spinning wheel.

"Now spin," said the king. "If you do not spin all this straw into gold by morning, you must die."

The king locked the door and went away.

Now the poor miller's daughter was all alone. She really did not know how to spin straw into gold. She did not know what to do. So she began to cry.

Suddenly the door opened, and a tiny
man came in. "Good evening, miller's da
he said. "Why are you crying?"

"Oh!" she said. "Oh! The king told
spin all this straw into gold. If it's no
morning, I must die!"

"What will you give me if I do it fo
little man asked.

"I will give you my necklace," said the
daughter.

The little man took the necklace. Then
down at the spinning wheel.

Whirl! Whirl! Whirl! Three times he w
the wheel and the work was done. Now tha
heap of straw was a heap of gold. And the li
man went away.

As soon as the sun was up, the king came i
He looked at the heap of gold. The king was
pleased.

"You have done well," he said to the miller'
daughter. "But I need more gold than that."

That evening the king took the miller's
daughter into a bigger room. There was nothin
in that room but a chair, a spinning wheel, and
great big heap of straw.

"Now spin," said the king. "If you do not
spin all this straw into gold by morning, you
must die."

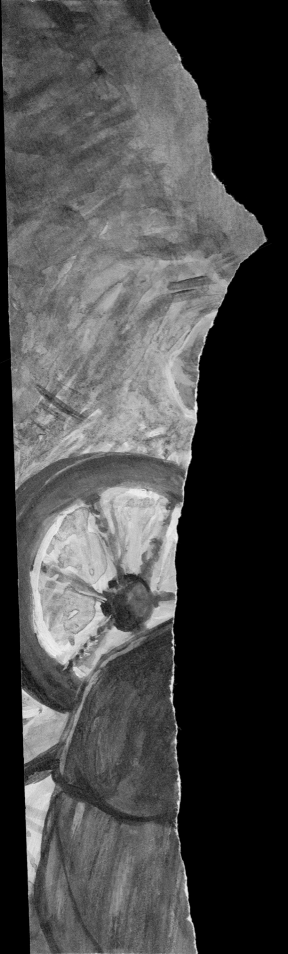

little
ughter,"

me to
t done by

r you?" the

miller's

he sat

hirled
t
ttle

n.

s

g
a

The king locked the door and went away.

Again the poor miller's daughter was all alone. She looked at all that straw. She did not know what to do. So she began to cry. Again the door opened and the little man came in.

"Good evening, miller's daughter," he said. "What will you give me if I spin all this straw into gold?"

"I will give you my ring," said the miller's daughter. The little man took the ring. Then he sat down at the spinning wheel.

Whirl! Whirl! Whirl! Three times he whirled the wheel and the work was done. Now that great big heap of straw was a great big heap of gold. And the little man went away.

As soon as the sun was up, the king came in. He looked at that great big heap of gold. The king was pleased.

"You have done well," he said to the miller's daughter. "But I need more gold than that."

That evening the king took the miller's daughter into a very big room. There was nothing in that room but a chair, a spinning wheel, and heaps and heaps of straw!

"Now spin," said the king. "If you spin all this straw into gold by morning, you will be my wife."

The king locked the door and went away.

When the miller's daughter was all alone, the little man came again. Again he said, "Good evening, miller's daughter. What will you give me if I spin this straw into gold?"

"I gave you my necklace," she said. "And I gave you my ring. I have nothing left to give you."

"Nothing?" the little man asked.

"Nothing," said the miller's daughter. And she began to cry.

"Don't cry, miller's daughter," the little man said. "I will help you. But you must promise to give me something . . ."

"Anything! Anything you ask!" she cried.

"Then promise me," the little man said. "Promise me that when you are queen you will give me your first baby."

"Yes! Yes! I promise!" said the miller's daughter. And she thought, "Who knows if I really shall be queen? And if I am queen, who knows if I shall have a baby?"

"Yes! Yes!" she said again. "I promise!"

The little man sat down at the spinning wheel. Whirl! Whirl! Whirl! Three times he whirled the wheel and the work was done. Now those heaps and heaps of straw were heaps and heaps of gold.

And the little man went away.

As soon as the sun was up the king came in. He looked at the heaps and heaps of gold. The king was very pleased.

He looked at the miller's beautiful daughter. "My dear," said the king. "We will be married this very day!" And so the miller's daughter became queen.

A year later, the king and the queen had a beautiful baby.

One evening the queen was in her room, playing with her baby. Suddenly, the little man came into her room.

"Good evening, queen," he said. "Now give me what you promised."

The queen had forgotten the little man. She had forgotten her promise, too.

"What promise?" she asked.

"You promised to give me your first baby," said the little man.

"I cannot give you my baby," said the queen. "I will give you my golden necklace." But the little man shook his head.

"I will give you my golden necklace and my beautiful golden ring," said the queen. But the little man shook his head.

"You may have all the riches of the kingdom," she said. "But let me keep my baby."

"No, queen," said the little man. "A baby is dearer to me than all the riches of the world."

The queen began to cry. The little man looked at the queen. "I will give you three days," he said. "If in three days you know my name, you may keep your baby.

"I will come every evening, for three evenings. Each time I will ask if you know my name."

And the little man went away.

That night the poor queen could not sleep. As soon as the sun was up, the queen called for her messenger. "Messenger," she said, "go through the town. Find out all the names people have. Come back before evening and tell them all to me."

That evening, the little man came into the queen's room.

"Good evening, queen," he said. "Do you know my name?"

The queen tried all the many names her messenger had found.

"Is it Al?" she asked.

"No," said the little man. "That's not my name."

"Is it Bill?"

"No."

"Is it Charlie?"

"No."

"Is it Dan?"

"No."

"Is it Ed?"

"No."

"Is it Fred?"

"No."

"Is it George?"

"No."

"Is it Henry?"

"No. No, no. That's not my name."

So they went, on and on and on. But all the little man said was: "No. No, no. That's not my name."

That very evening, as soon as the little man had gone away, the queen called for her messenger. "Messenger," she said, "go through the kingdom. Find out all the strange names people have. Come back tomorrow, before evening, and tell them all to me. Hurry."

On the second evening the little man came into the queen's room.

"Good evening, queen," he said. "Do you know my name?"

The queen asked him all the strange names her messenger had found.

"Bump-on-a-lump?" she asked.

"No," said the little man. "That's not my name."

"Is it Diddle Dump?"

"No."

"Is it Bottom?"

"No."

"Is it Top?"

"No."

"Is it Skip?"

"No."

"Is it Hop?"

"No."

"Is it Goldie Locks?"

"No."

"Is it Lucky Fox?"

"No."

"Is it Bluster Beast?"

"No. No, no. That's not my name."

So they went, on and on and on.

But all the little man said was: "No. No, no. That's not my name."

That evening, as soon as the little man had gone away, the queen called for her messenger. "Messenger," she said. "Go once more through the kingdom. You must find more names for me! Come back tomorrow, before evening, and tell them all to me. Hurry!"

On the third day, it was almost evening when the messenger came back.

"I could not find any new names for you," he said.

"Not any new names?" asked the queen. "Not any new names at all?"

"Well," said the messenger. "I did find something. Something very strange . . ."

"Tell me," said the queen. "And hurry!"

So the messenger told the queen what he had found.

"Last night," he said, "I went up high, high into the mountains. I went deep into the woods where the fox and the hare say good night to each other. There I saw a little house. In front of that little house there was a fire. And around that little fire a tiny little man was dancing. While he was dancing, he was singing:

> Tonight my cakes I bake.
> Tonight my drink I make.
> Tomorrow, tomorrow, tomorrow
> The queen's little baby I take
> Lucky I'll go as lucky I came
> for
>
> R U M P E L S T I L T S K I N
>
> is my name!

How happy the queen was to hear that name! Now it was the third evening, and the little man came again.

"Good evening, queen," he said. "Do you know my name?"

"Tell me, is it Tom?" the queen asked.

"No."

"Hm . . . let me see. Is it Dick?"

"No."

"Well, let me think . . . Is it Harry?"

"No." The little man laughed and he shook his head.

"No, no. That's not my name."

"Then . . . tell me . . ." asked the queen.

"Could it be . . .?

Is it . . .

perhaps . . .

RUMPELSTILTSKIN?"

How angry the little man was!

"Someone must have told you!" he cried. "Who told you?"

He stamped so hard with his right foot that he made a deep hole in the floor. Oh, he was angry! He stamped hard with his left foot, too. And he fell deep into the earth. No one has seen him since.

Think About It

1. How did the miller's daughter get into trouble in the first place?
2. Tell how the little man helped the miller's daughter and what she had to do to thank him.
3. How did the queen save her first baby from the little man?
4. What lesson might be learned from this story?

Explore   Search other books and stories for the funniest, longest, or weirdest person's name you can find. Some suggestions on where to look are fairy tales, folktales, encyclopedias, and fiction stories.

Create and Share   List the name you found on the chalkboard under Funniest, Longest, Weirdest. Have your classmates do the same. Then hold a contest for the classroom winner in each category.

My Other Name

Jennifer's my other name
(It's make-believe
and just a game.)
I'm really Anne,
But just the same
I'd much
much
rather
have a name
like Jennifer.

(So, if you can
don't call me Anne.)

—*Myra Cohn Livingston*

Ali Baba Bernstein

by Johanna Hurwitz

Part 1

David Bernstein was eight years, five months, and seventeen days old when he chose his new name.

There were already four Davids in David Bernsteins's third-grade class. Every time his teacher, Mrs. Booxbaum, called. "David" all four boys answered. David didn't like that one bit. He wished he had an exciting name like one of the explorers he learned about in social studies— Vasco da Gama. Once he found two unusual names on a program his parents brought home from a concert—Zubin Mehta and Wolfgang Amadeus Mozart. Now those were names with pizzazz!

David Bernstein might have gone along forever being just another David if it had not been for the book report that his teacher gave for homework.

"I will give extra credit for fat books," Mrs. Booxbaum told the class.

She didn't realize that all of her students would try to outdo one another. That afternoon when the third grade went to the school library, everyone tried to find the fattest book.

Melanie found a book with eighty pages. Jeffrey found a book with one hundred nineteen pages. David K. and David S. each took a copy of the same book. It had one hundred forty-five pages.

None of the books were long enough for David Bernstein. He wanted a book that had more pages than the total of all the pages in all the books his classmates were reading. He wanted to be the best student in the class—even in the entire school.

That afternoon he asked his mother what the fattest book was. Mrs. Bernstein thought for a minute. "I guess that would have to be the Manhattan telephone book," she said.

David Bernstein rushed to get the phone book. He lifted it up and opened to the last page. When he saw that it had over 1,578 pages, he was delighted.

He knew that no student in the history of the school had ever read such a fat book. Just think how much extra credit he would get! David took the book and began to read name after name after name. After turning through all the *A* pages, he skipped to the name Bernstein. He found the listing for his father, Robert Bernstein. There were fifteen of them. Then he counted the number of David Bernsteins in the telephone book. There were seventeen. There was also a woman named Davida and a man named Davis, but he didn't count them. Right at that moment, David Bernstein decided two things: he would change his name and he would find another book to read.

The next day David went back to the school library. He asked the librarian to help him pick out a very fat book. "But it must be very exciting, too," he told her.

"I know just the thing for you," said the librarian.

She handed David a thick book with a bright red cover. It was *The Arabian Nights*. It had only three hundred thirty-seven pages, but it looked a lot more interesting than the phone book. David checked the book out of the library and spent the entire evening reading it. When he showed the book to his teacher the next day, she was very pleased.

"That is a good book," she said. "David, you have made a fine choice."

It was at that moment that David Bernstein announced his new name. He had found it in the library book.

"From now on," David said, "I want to be called Ali Baba Bernstein." Mrs. Booxbaum was surprised. David's parents were even more surprised.

"David is a beautiful name," said his mother. "It was my grandfather's name."

"You can't just go around changing your name when you feel like it," his father said. "How will I ever know who I'm talking to?"

"You'll know it's still me," Ali Baba told his parents.

Mr. and Mrs. Bernstein finally agreed, although both of them sometimes forgot and called their son David.

So now in Mrs. Booxbaum's class, there were three Davids and one Ali Baba. Ali Baba Bernstein was very happy. He was sure that a boy with an exciting name would have truly exciting adventures.

Part II

When Ali Baba Bernstein was eight years, eleven months, and four days old, his mother asked him how he wanted to celebrate his ninth birthday. Ali Baba wanted to do something different.

"Do you remember when I counted all the David Bernsteins in the telephone book?"

Mrs. Bernstein nodded.

"I'd like to meet them all," said David. I want to invite them here for my birthday."

"But you don't know them," his mother said. "And they are not your age."

"I want to see what they are all like," said Ali Baba.

That night Ali Baba's parents talked about the David Bernstein Party. Mr. Bernstein liked his son's idea. He thought the other David Bernsteins might be curious to meet one another. So it was agreed that Ali Baba would have the party he wanted.

The very next morning, which was Saturday, Ali Baba and his father went to his father's office. Ali Baba had written an invitation to the David Bernstein party.

Dear David Bernstein:

I found your name in the Manhattan telephone book. My name is David Bernstein, too. I want to meet all the David Bernsteins in New York. I am having a party on Friday, May 12th at 7:00 P.M., and I hope you can come.

My mother is cooking supper. She is a good cook.

Yours truly,

David Bernstein

(also known as Ali Baba Bernstein)

P.S. May 12th is my ninth birthday, but you don't have to bring a present.

RSVP: 211-3579.

Mr. Bernstein had explained that RSVP was a French abbreviation that meant please tell me if you are going to come. He also said that his son should give his age in the letter.

That evening Ali Baba addressed the
seventeen envelopes so that the invitations could
be mailed on Monday morning. His father
supplied the stamps. By the end of the week, two
David Bernsteins had already called to say they
would come.

By the time Ali Baba Bernstein was eight
years, eleven months, and twenty-nine days old,
seven David Bernsteins had said they would
come to the party. Four David Bernsteins called to
say they couldn't come.

Six David Bernsteins did not answer at all. The
evening of the party finally arrived.

Ali Baba had decided to wear a pair of slacks,
a sport jacket, and real dress shoes.

Ali Baba was surprised when the first David
arrived in a jogging suit and running shoes.

"How do you do," he said when Ali Baba
opened the door. "I'm David Bernstein."

"Of course," said the birthday boy. "Call me Ali Baba."

Soon the living room was filled with David Bernsteins. They ranged in age from exactly nine years and three hours old to seventy-six years old. There was a television director, a grocery store owner, a mailman, an animal groomer, a dentist, a high-school teacher, and a writer. They all lived in Manhattan now, but they had been born in different places. None of them had ever met any of the others before.

All of the Davids enjoyed the dinner.

"David, will you please pass those delicious rolls," asked the mailman.

"Of course, David," said the animal groomer on his left.

"David, would you please pass the pitcher of apple cider this way," asked the dentist.

"Here it is, David," said the television director.

"I have trouble remembering names," the seventy-six-year-old David Bernstein told Ali Baba. "At this party I can't possibly forget." He smiled at Ali Baba. "What did you say your nickname was?"

"Ali Baba is not a nickname. I have chosen it to be my real name. There are too many David Bernsteins. There were even more in the telephone book who didn't come tonight."

"I was the only David Bernstein to finish the New York City Marathon," said David Bernstein the dentist. He was the one wearing running shoes.

"The poodles I clip don't care what my name is," said David Bernstein the animal groomer.

"It's not what you're called but what you do that matters," said the seventy-six-year-old David Bernstein.

All of them agreed to that.

"I once read that in some places children are given temporary names. They call them 'milk names.' They can then choose whatever names they want when they get older," said David Bernstein the delicatessen owner. "Just because we all have the same name doesn't make us the same."

"You're right," agreed David Bernstein the mailman.

"Here, here," called out David Bernstein the television director. He raised his glass of apple cider. "A toast to the youngest David Bernstein in the room."

Everyone turned to Ali Baba. He was about to say that he didn't want to be called David. But somehow he didn't mind his name so much now that he had met all these other David Bernsteins. They *were* all different. There would never be another David Bernstein like himself. One of these days he might go back to calling himself David again. But not just now.

Think About It

1. How did the Anne in the poem and the David in the story feel about their names? What did each of them do about their names?

2. Why did David want to be different? What parts of the story tell you about this?

3. How did meeting the other David Bernsteins change David's feeling about his own name?

4. The oldest David Bernstein told Ali Baba, "It's not what you're called but what you do that matters." Do you think this is true? Why or why not?

5. From the stories you read in YOU NAME IT!, what did you find out about names?

Create and Share   Make a name tag
giving yourself a new first name. Wear it for a while. Tell why you picked that name and how your friends felt about your changing your name.

Explore   Look up your family name in the telephone book. Tell what you found there.

D.E.A.R.
Drop Everything And Read

First, I saw Matilda reading a book.
She was learning to fish and was
     baiting her hook.

Next, I saw Bartholomew reading a book.
He was wearing an apron while
     learning to cook.

Then, I saw Lucinda reading a book.
She was very involved and found her
     own little nook.

Last, I saw Billy Bob reading a book.
He was looking for clues and then
     chasing a crook.

Now I see you and you're reading a book.
What are you learning? Do you mind if
     I look?

Ramona Reads

from RAMONA QUIMBY, AGE 8
by Beverly Cleary

Being a member of the Quimby family in the
third grade was harder than Ramona had
expected. Her father was often tired, in a hurry,
or studying on the dining-room table, which
meant no one could disturb him by watching
television. At school she was still not sure how
she felt about Mrs. Whaley. Liking a teacher was
important, Ramona had discovered when she was
in the first grade.

Those were the bad parts of the third grade.
There were good parts, too. Ramona enjoyed
riding the bus to school, and she enjoyed keeping
Yard Ape from getting the best of her. Then
another good part of the third grade began the
second week of school.

Just before her class was to make its weekly
visit to the school library, Mrs. Whaley
announced, "Today and from now on we are
going to have Sustained Silent Reading every
day."

Ramona liked the sound of Sustained Silent Reading, even though she was not sure what it meant, because it sounded important.

Mrs. Whaley continued. "This means that every day after lunch we are going to sit at our desks and read silently to ourselves any book we choose in the library."

"Even mysteries?" someone asked.

"Even mysteries," said Mrs. Whaley.

"Do we have to give book reports on what we read?" asked one suspicious member of the class.

"No book reports on your Sustained Silent Reading books," Mrs. Whaley promised the class. Then she went on, "I don't think Sustained Silent Reading sounds very interesting, so I think we will call it something else." Here she printed four big letters on the blackboard, and as she pointed she read out, "*D. E. A. R.* Can anyone guess what these letters stand for?"

The class thought and thought.

"Do Everything All Right," suggested someone. A good thought, but not the right answer.

"Don't Eat A Reader," suggested Yard Ape. Mrs. Whaley laughed and told him to try again.

As Ramona thought, she stared out the window at the blue sky, the treetops, and, in the distance, the snow-capped peak of Mount Hood looking like a giant licked ice-cream cone. *R.* could stand for *Run* and *A* for *And.* "Drop Everything And Run," Ramona burst out. Mrs. Whaley laughed and said, "Almost right, Ramona, but have you forgotten we are talking about reading?"

"Drop Everything And Read!" chorused the rest of the class. Ramona felt silly. She should have thought of that herself.

Ramona decided that she preferred Sustained Silent Reading to DEAR because it sounded more grown-up. When time came for everyone to Drop Everything And Read, she sat quietly doing her Sustained Silent Reading.

How peaceful it was to be left alone in school. She could read without trying to hide her book under her desk or behind a bigger book. She was not expected to write lists of words she did not know, so she could figure them out by skipping and guessing. Mrs. Whaley did not expect the class to write summaries of what they read either, so she did not have to choose easy books to make sure she would get her summary right. Now if Mrs. Whaley would leave her alone to draw, too, school would be almost perfect.

Yes, Sustained Silent Reading was the best part of the day.

The next morning Ramona stayed home from school. During the night, she had gotten sick. She was lying on the couch when Picky-picky the cat strolled into the living room. He stared at Ramona as if he felt she did not belong on the couch.

A funny man appeared on the TV screen. He had eaten a pizza, which had given him indigestion. He groaned. "I can't believe I ate the *whole* thing."

The next commercial showed a cat stepping back and forth in a little dance. "Do you think we could train Picky-picky to do that?" Ramona asked her mother.

Mrs. Quimby was amused at the idea of old Picky-picky dancing. "I doubt it," she said. "That cat isn't really dancing. They just turn the film back and forth so it looks as if he's dancing."

Late that afternoon Ramona was awakened by the doorbell. Was it someone interesting? She hoped so, for she was bored. The visitor turned out to be Sara.

"Hi, Sara," said Ramona with the weakest smile she could manage.

"Mrs. Whaley said to tell you this book is not for DEAR. This one is for a book report," Sara explained from the doorway.

Ramona groaned.

"She said to tell you," Sara continued, "that she wants us to stand up in front of the class and pretend we are selling the book. She doesn't want us to tell the whole story. She says she has already heard all the stories quite a few times."

Ramona felt worse. Not only would she have to give a book report, she would have to listen to twenty-five book reports given by other people, another reason for wanting to stay home.

When Sara left, Ramona examined the big envelope she had brought.

Then her sister Beezus arrived with an armload of books that she dropped on a chair. "Homework!" she said and groaned.

"My class is giving book reports," she informed Beezus, so her sister would know she had schoolwork to do, too. "We have to pretend to sell a book to someone."

"We did that a couple of times," said Beezus. "Teachers always tell you not to tell the whole story, and half the kids finish by saying, 'If you want to know what happens next, read the book, and somebody always says, 'Read this book, or I'll punch you in the nose.' "

Ramona, still feeling weak, moped around the house for another day worrying about her book report. If she made it interesting, Mrs. Whaley would think she was showing off. If she did not make it interesting, her teacher would not like it.

Suddenly Ramona decided she had to think of a way to make it interesting.

The book, *The Left-Behind Cat*, which Mrs. Whaley had sent home for Ramona to read for her report, was divided into chapters but used babyish words. The story was about a cat that was left behind when a family moved away and about its adventures with a dog, another cat, and some children before it finally found a home with a nice old couple who gave it a saucer of cream and named it Lefty because its left paw was white and because it had been left behind.

Medium-boring, thought Ramona, good enough to pass the time on the bus, but not good enough to read during Sustained Silent Reading. Besides, cream cost too much to give to a cat. The most the old people would give a cat was half-and-half, she thought. Ramona required accuracy from books as well as from people.

"Daddy, how do you sell something?" Ramona interrupted her father, who was studying, even though she knew she should not. However, her need for an answer was urgent.

Mr. Quimby did not look up from his book. "You ought to know. You see enough commercials on television."

Ramona considered his answer. She had always looked upon commercials as entertainment, but now she thought about some of her favorites—the cat that danced back and forth, the dog that pushed away brand-X dog food with his paw, the man who ate a pizza, got indigestion, and groaned that he couldn't believe he ate the *whole* thing.

"Do you mean I should do a book report like a TV commercial?" Ramona asked.

"Why not?" Mr. Quimby answered. "Your teacher told you to pretend you're selling the book, so sell it. What better way than a TV commercial?"

Ramona went to her room and looked at her table, which the family called "Ramona's studio," because it was a clutter of crayons, different kinds of paper, Scotch tape, bits of yarn, and odds and ends that Ramona used for amusing herself. Then Ramona thought a moment, and then suddenly she went to work. She knew exactly what she wanted to do and set about doing it. She worked with paper, crayons, Scotch tape, and rubber bands. She worked so hard and with such pleasure that her cheeks grew pink. Nothing in the whole world felt as good as being able to make something from a sudden idea.

Finally, with a big sigh of relief, Ramona leaned back in her chair to admire her work: three cat masks with holes for eyes and mouths, masks that could be worn by hooking rubber bands over ears. But Ramona did not stop there. With pencil and paper, she began to write out what she would say. She was so full of ideas that she printed rather than waste time in cursive writing. Next she phoned Sara and Janet, keeping her voice low and trying not to giggle so she wouldn't disturb her father any more than necessary, and explained her plan to them. Both her friends giggled and agreed to take part in the book report. Ramona spent the rest of the evening memorizing what she was going to say.

The next morning Ramona waited for book reports to begin.

After arithmetic, Mrs. Whaley called on several people to come to the front of the room to pretend they were selling books to the class. Most of the reports began, "This is a book about . . ." and many, as Beezus had predicted, ended with ". . . if you want to find out what happens next, read the book."

Then Mrs. Whaley said, "We have time for one more report before lunch. Who wants to be next?"

Ramona waved her hand, and Mrs. Whaley nodded.

Ramona beckoned to Sara and Janet, who
giggled in an embarrassed way but joined
Ramona, standing behind her and off to one side.
All three girls slipped on their cat masks and
giggled again. Ramona took a deep breath as
Sara and Janet began to chant, *"Meow,* meow,
meow, meow. *Meow,* meow, meow, meow," and
danced back and forth like the cat they had seen
in the cat-food commercial on television.

"*Left-Behind Cat* gives kids something to smile
about," said Ramona in a loud clear voice, while
her chorus meowed softly behind her. She
wasn't sure that what she said was exactly true,
but neither were the commercials that showed
cats eating dry cat food without making any noise.

"Kids who have tried *Left-Behind Cat* are all
smiles, smiles, smiles. *Left-Behind Cat* is the book
kids ask for by name. Kids can read it every day
and thrive on it. The happiest kids read *Left-
Behind Cat*. *Left-Behind Cat* contains cats, dogs,
people—" Here Ramona caught sight of Yard Ape
leaning back in his seat, grinning. She could not
help interrupting herself with a giggle, and after
suppressing it she tried not to look at Yard Ape
and to take up where she had left off. ". . . cats,
dogs, people—" The giggle came back, and
Ramona was lost. She could not remember what
came next. ". . . cats, dogs, people," she
repeated, trying to start and failing.

Mrs. Whaley and the class waited. Yard Ape grinned. Ramona's loyal chorus meowed and danced. This performance could not go on all morning. Ramona had to say something, anything to end the waiting, the meowing, her book report. She tried desperately to recall a cat-food commercial, any cat-food commercial, and could not. All she could remember was the man on the television who ate the pizza, and so she blurted out the only sentence she could think of, "I can't believe I read the *whole* thing!"

Mrs. Whaley's laugh rang out above the laughter of the class. Ramona felt her face turn red behind her mask, and her ears, visible to the class, turned red as well.

"Thank you, Ramona," said Mrs. Whaley. "That was most entertaining. Class, you are excused for lunch."

Ramona snatched up her lunch box and went jumping down the stairs to the cafeteria. She laughed to herself because she knew exactly what all the boys and girls from her class would say when they finished their lunches. She knew because she planned to say it herself. "I can't believe I ate the *whole* thing!"

Friends for Life

by Judy Blume

When I was small my mother took me to the public library in Elizabeth, New Jersey, where I would sit on the floor and browse among the books. I not only liked the pictures and the stories, but also the feel and the smell of the books themselves.

My favorite book was *Madeline*, by Ludwig Bemelmans. I loved that book! I loved it so much that I hid it in my toy drawer so my mother wouldn't be able to return it to the library. Even after the overdue notices came I didn't tell my mother where the book was. If only I had asked, I'm sure she would have bought me my own copy, but I didn't know then that was a possibility. I thought the copy I had hidden was the only copy in the whole world. I knew it was wrong to hide the book, but there was no way I was going to part with *Madeline*. I memorized the words in the book, and though I couldn't really read, I pretended that I could.

When I did learn to read I was very proud. Not only could I read *Madeline*, but I could read the back of the cereal box, just like my older brother. When I visited my aunt and uncle I was allowed to take their beautifully illustrated copy of *Mother Goose* from the bookshelf—as long as I washed my hands first—and I would read the nursery rhymes on my own. In school we were divided into reading groups with bird names. I was a bluejay in first grade and a robin in second.

But the stories in our readers weren't nearly as much fun as the stories in the books I chose myself. I loved getting into bed at night with a favorite book and reading until my father said it was time to put out my light.

I read all the Oz books, the Nancy Drew mysteries, and the Betsy-Tacy books by Maud Hart Lovelace. When I was older, in junior high, I discovered the books on my parents' bookshelves. No one ever told me what books I could read or what books I couldn't. Books opened up a whole new world to me. Through them I discovered new ideas, traveled to new places, and met new people. Books helped me learn to understand other people and they taught me a lot about myself.

It's more than forty years since I hid that copy of *Madeline,* and I've never done that again, but I can still recite the story by heart. And when my daughter was born, *Madeline* was the first book I bought for her. Betsy and Tacy are still alive in my mind, and when I close my eyes I can picture them on a summer day as they call on their neighbor Tib. Some books you never forget. Some characters become your friends for life.

I loved getting lost in books when I was young. I still do!

The Pain and the Great One

by Judy Blume

In Friends for Life, *Judy Blume tells the story of how her love for books developed. She wrote that she loved getting lost in books and still does. Now she not only reads them, she writes them. The Pain and the Great One is a book she wrote; one you may not forget.*

The Pain

My brother's a Pain. He won't get out of bed in the morning. Mom has to carry him into the kitchen. He opens his eyes when he smells his corn flakes.

He should get dressed himself.

He's six. He's in first grade. But he's so pokey Daddy has to help him or he'd never be ready in time and he'd miss the bus.

He cries if I leave without him. Then Mom gets mad and yells at me, which is another reason why my brother's a pain.

He's got to be first to show Mom his school work. She says *ooh* and *aah* over all his pictures, which aren't great at all, but just ordinary first grade stuff.

At dinner he picks at his food. He's not supposed to get dessert if he doesn't eat his meat. But he always gets it anyway.

When he takes a bath my brother the Pain powders the whole bathroom and never get his face clean. Daddy says he's learning to take care of himself. I say, he's a slob!

My brother the Pain is two years younger than me. So how come he gets to stay up as late as I do? Which isn't really late enough for somebody in third grade anyway.

I asked Mom and Daddy about that.

They said, "You're right. You *are* older. You *should* stay up later."

So they tucked the Pain into bed. I couldn't wait for the fun to begin. I waited and waited and waited. But Daddy and Mom just sat there reading books.

Finally I shouted, "I'm going to bed!"

"We thought you wanted to stay up later," they said.

"I did. But without the Pain there's nothing to do!"

"Remember that tomorrow," Mom said. And she smiled.

But the next day my brother was a Pain again.

When I got a phone call he danced all around me singing stupid songs at the top of his lungs. Why does he have to act that way?

And why does he always want to be garbage
man when I build a city out of blocks?

Who needs him knocking down buildings
with his dumb old trucks!

And I would really like to know why the cat
sleeps on the Pain's bed instead of mine
especially since I am the one who feeds her. That
is the meanest thing of all!

I don't understand how Mom can say the Pain
is lovable. She's always kissing him and hugging
him and doing disgusting things like that. And
Daddy says the Pain is just
what they always wanted.

YUCK!

I think they love
him better than me.

The Great One

My sister thinks she's so great just because she's older which makes Daddy and Mom think she's really smart. But I know the truth. My sister's a jerk.

She thinks she's great just because she can play the piano and you can tell the songs are real ones. But I like my songs better even if nobody has ever heard them before.

My sister thinks she's so great just because she can work the can opener, which means she gets to feed the cat. The cat likes her better than me just because she feeds her.

My sister thinks she's so great just because Aunt Diana lets her watch the baby and tells her how much the baby likes her.

All the time the baby is sleeping in my dresser drawer, which Mom has fixed up like a bed for when the baby comes to visit. I'm not supposed to touch him even if he's in *my* drawer and gets changed on *my* bed.

My sister thinks she's so great just because she can remember phone numbers. When she dials she never gets the wrong person.

When she has friends over they build whole cities out of blocks. I like to be garbage man. I zoom my trucks all around. So what if I knock down some of their buildings?

"It's not fair that she always gets to use the blocks!"

I told Daddy and Mom. They said, "You're right. Today you can use the blocks all by yourself."

"I'm going to build a whole city without you!" I told the Great One. "Go ahead," she said. "Go build a whole state without me. See if I care!"

So I did. I built a whole country all by myself. Only it's not the funnest thing to play blocks alone. When I zoomed my trucks and knocked down buildings nobody cared but me!

"Remember that tomorrow," Mom said, when I told her I was through playing blocks.

The next day we went swimming. I can't stand my sister when we go swimming. She thinks she's so great just because she can swim and dive and isn't afraid to put her face in the water. I'm scared to put mine in so she calls me *baby*, which is why I have to spit water at her and pull her hair and even pinch her sometimes.

I don't think it's fair for Daddy and Mom to yell at me because none of it's my fault. But they yell anyway.

Then Mom hugs my sister and messes with her hair and does other disgusting things like that. Daddy says the Great One is just what they always wanted.

YUCK!

I think they love her better than me.

Think About It

1. What's the connection between liking to read when you're young and writing good stories and poems when you're older?
2. Does Judy Blume say anything about books that reminds you of yourself?
3. Do you agree with the Pain or the Great One? Explain.
4. Explain what you think the Pain and the Great One might learn if they read what the other one wrote.

Create and Share
You read what the Pain thinks, and you read what the Great One thinks. Now write what Mom and Dad think. Use details from the story.

Explore
Find another one of Judy Blume's books to read. One that is a lot like *The Pain and the Great One* is *Tales of a Fourth Grade Nothing*.

The Magic Bookshelf

by Patricia Clapp

Characters

SALLY	ALICE IN WONDERLAND
TIM	DOROTHY OF OZ
FAIRY GODFATHER	CHRISTOPHER ROBIN
CINDERELLA	RED RIDING HOOD
PETER PAN	JACK THE GIANT KILLER

(*As curtain rises*, SALLY *is reading to Tim.*)

SALLY: (*Reading*) "—and when the Prince tried the glass slipper on Cinderella's foot, it fit perfectly! Taking her hand he helped her to her feet and said—"

TIM: I'm tired of being read to! I wish I could go out.

SALLY: You know you can't go out. You're just getting over measles.

TIM: I'm tired of having measles, and I'm tired of hearing about silly Cinderella! I wish I had real, live people to play with. The only good part is the Fairy Godmother. I wish *I* had one.

SALLY: You'd have to be *really* miserable, just like Cinderella.

TIM: I *am* really miserable! My measles hurt!

SALLY: Measles can't hurt! You're just pretending!

TIM: I am not! I'm *very* miserable and I'm suffering like anything! Please, Fairy Godmother, please come and help me! (FAIRY GODFATHER *suddenly appears in the doorway.*)

FAIRY GODFATHER: Since you put it like that—

TIM: Who are you?

SALLY: Where did you come from?

FAIRY GODFATHER: I'm Tim's Fairy Godfather, and I came from—well, never mind where I came from.

TIM: I don't have a Fairy Godfather!

FAIRY GODFATHER: Now there's a ridiculous statement if ever I heard one! I'm standing right here in front of him, and he says he doesn't have a Fairy Godfather! Now, Tim, just why did you call me?

TIM: I didn't know I was calling you.

FAIRY GODFATHER: You were saying you were miserable, and calling for me.

SALLY: But Tim wasn't really miserable; that was just pretend.

FAIRY GODFATHER: Well, I'm just pretend, too.

SALLY: But I can see you!

FAIRY GODFATHER: Of course, I'm right here!

TIM: Then why did you say you were just pretend?

FAIRY GODFATHER: (*Shaking his head*) What's the matter with you two? Don't you know there is *real* pretend as well as *pretend* pretend?

TIM: No, what's the difference?

FAIRY GODFATHER: It's perfectly plain. *Real* pretend things are fairies, and wishing wells, and magic and flying around the room. *Pretend* pretend things are the horses on merry-go-rounds and marshmallow bananas, and things like *that!* Do you understand?

TIM: I think so.

FAIRY GODFATHER: Good! Now, let's get down to business. What did you call me for? I haven't all day, you know.

SALLY: He was tired of listening to me read and he wanted someone to play with.

TIM: Cinderella! All that dopey stuff about Prince Charming and pumpkin coaches. Everyone knows you can't ride in a pumpkin.

FAIRY GODFATHER: I suppose everyone knows there aren't Fairy Godfathers, too!

TIM: Oh, sorry.

FAIRY GODFATHER: That's better. So—you wanted someone to play with, did you? What's wrong with storybook people?

TIM: I wanted a real person to play games with.

FAIRY GODFATHER: There you go again! Real—pretend—you still don't know the difference! I can see I'm going to have to do something about this. (*He rises and looks at the titles of books on the shelf.*) Let's see. How about Peter Pan to start with?

TIM: To start what with?

FAIRY GODFATHER: To start playing with, of course! You *did* want someone to play with.

SALLY: I think Tim means he wants some real, live children, to play games with, like pirates.

FAIRY GODFATHER: You can't beat Peter Pan when it comes to playing pirates. You do remember about him and Captain Hook, don't you?

TIM: No, I don't think I do.

FAIRY GODFATHER: You mean you never read about Peter Pan?

SALLY: Tim doesn't like books much.

FAIRY GODFATHER: Well! Where do you think *I* came from? You read about Cinderella having a Fairy Godmother and you wanted one, didn't you?

TIM: Yes.

FAIRY GODFATHER: So you called me. And I came. Here I am. Now! Wasn't that out of a book?

TIM: Yes, I guess it was.

FAIRY GODFATHER: All right, then! Let's have no more nonsense about book people not being real! (*He takes the book* Peter Pan *from the shelf, and lightly taps the cover.*)
Peter, Peter, in the book,
Come out and give our Tim a look!

(**PETER PAN** *comes through the door.*)

PETER PAN: Somebody call me?

SALLY: Peter Pan!

PETER PAN: (*Making a bow*) At your service!

TIM: It can't be!

FAIRY GODFATHER: And why can't it be?

TIM: Peter Pan is just somebody in a book!

PETER PAN: (*To Fairy Godfather*) What's he talking about?

FAIRY GODFATHER: It's a very sad case! This boy, Tim, doesn't believe in book people!

PETER PAN: (*Shocked*) No!

FAIRY GODFATHER: That's right. He thinks that just because he *reads* about us, we're not real!

PETER PAN: (*To Tim*) Pinch me! (*TIM pinches him.*) Ouch! There! Am I real or not?

TIM: You *feel* real.

PETER PAN: I should hope so! Look! I *am* real. We're *real* pretend, and that's the realest kind of real there is!

SALLY: Are there more of you?

PETER PAN: Are there more—? (*To Fairy Godfather*)
Are there more of us, she wants to know!
Come on, old-timer, show her!

FAIRY GODFATHER: Well, how about—

SALLY: (*Holding out the book she was reading*) I want
to see Cinderella!

FAIRY GODFATHER: (*Tapping on the cover*)
Cinderella in the book,
Come, let Sally take a look.
(CINDERELLA *comes through the door.*)

SALLY: (*Joyfully*) Cinderella!

CINDERELLA: Hello, Sally.

FAIRY GODFATHER: You know one another?

CINDERELLA: We've never really met before, but
Sally and I are old friends. She's always
reading about me.

SALLY: I read about you to Tim today, but I don't
think he really—well—believed in you.

CINDERELLA: This is terrible! Imagine not having
people believe in you! What can we do to
prove we're really us?

PETER PAN: I know. Let's have a meeting! Old-
timer, you stand there by the bookshelf
and call some of the others in. Who's there?

FAIRY GODFATHER: (*At bookcase, scanning the titles*)
There's Alice in Wonderland.

CINDERELLA: Oh, she's lots of fun! Ask her—I
haven't seen her in ages!

FAIRY GODFATHER: (*Taking a book from the shelf*)
Alice, Alice in the book—

PETER PAN: Do it the short way.

FAIRY GODFATHER: Very well, then. (*He runs his
hand lightly over the backs of many books.*)
Everyone within a book,
Give Tim and Sally both a look!

(PETER PAN *and* CINDERELLA *take turns announcing.*)

CINDERELLA: Miss Alice, from Wonderland!

ALICE: Cinderella! How nice to see you!

PETER PAN: Master Jack, Killer of Giants!

JACK: Hi, Pete—how's Wendy?

CINDERELLA: Miss Dorothy, from the Land of Oz!

DOROTHY: Why, hello! For a minute I thought I was
   back in the cyclone, being whooshed into Oz!
   Is this a party?

CINDERELLA: No, a meeting. We'll explain soon.

PETER PAN: Christopher Robin, and Pooh Bear!

CHRISTOPHER ROBIN: Are we in time for tea? Pooh is rather hungry.

CINDERELLA: Maybe later, Christopher Robin; not just now. (**RED RIDING HOOD** *runs in*.) Ah, here's Red Riding Hood. Don't *rush so,* dear!

RED RIDING HOOD: I can't help it! It's that dreadful Wolf! He keeps following me!

ALICE: Will somebody please tell me what we're doing here? I can't stay very long. The Queen is having another of her tea parties.

PETER PAN: (*Clapping his hands*) Now, the reason we're all here is that these two—(*Pointing to Sally and Tim*)—don't believe in book people!

JACK: They *don't.*

PETER PAN: (*Shaking his head*) No, they don't!

FAIRY GODFATHER: It started when Tim wished I would appear and bring him someone to play with. Naturally, I did. He wanted playmates, and I invited you to come and play with him.

JACK: Here we are—what shall we play?

PETER PAN: That comes later. First we have to prove to Tim that we're real pretenders. Has anyone a suggestion?

ALICE: (*Standing and addressing Tim*) What makes you think we're not real?

TIM: Well, when Sally and I were little, Mother and Daddy used to read to us.

CHRISTOPHER ROBIN: Yes?

TIM: They used to read about Jack and Jill and Peter Rabbit and Sleeping Beauty and all those things—er—people. Mother and Daddy said that they were just made-up stories about made-up things—er, people and animals—and that they didn't really happen. That they were fairy tales!

JACK: Of course. You see, there are some things that grownups don't know.

SALLY: There are?

DOROTHY: Yes, and it's too bad, really, because they're very important things.

TIM: Like what?

RED RIDING HOOD: Like what kind of noise the grass makes when it's growing, and whether there really is a pot of gold at the end of the rainbow.

TIM: There is, isn't there?

ALICE: Of course! But the most important thing they don't know is about real pretenders.

SALLY: I thought grownups knew everything.

FAIRY GODFATHER: They know a great many things —but some of the most important things they ever knew, they've forgotten!

TIM: You mean the pretend things?

PETER: That's right. They *used* to know, because all children are part fairy themselves, and fairies know all about pretend.

CINDERELLA: But somehow, as grownups get older, they forget. It's very sad, and yet it almost always happens.

SALLY: Oh, I don't want to grow up and forget!

DOROTHY: There *is* a way to keep the magic that children and fairies know about.

SALLY: Oh, how? Please tell.

FAIRY GODFATHER: Read! Read and read and read until you've stored up so much magic and pretend and make-believe that you can never lose it all. Read fairy tales and nursery rhymes and children's books.

ALICE: Read about animals that talk—like the White Rabbit.

CHRISTOPHER ROBIN: Read about toys that are alive—like Pooh Bear.

CINDERELLA: Read about Fairy Godmothers like mine.

JACK: Read my story about giants!

FAIRY GODFATHER: Read about them all until they're a part of you that you won't ever lose. Read about them until they are your friends and playmates. Read about them until you can never be lonely and never be bored and never forget!

SALLY: Will it work?

FAIRY GODFATHER: I said it would, didn't I? (*Turning to the storybook people*) Am I right?

ALL: Yes! Yes!

PETER PAN: You can read about anything you like. Whatever sort of friend you want, you'll find in a book. We're always there—we never go away.

FAIRY GODFATHER: (*To Tim*) Do you believe in us?

TIM: Oh, *yes!*

FAIRY GODFATHER: And you won't forget?

TIM: Oh, *no*, sir!

FAIRY GODFATHER: Now it's time for us to go.
We're all very busy, and we must get back to
our chores. Come along, everybody.
(*The storybook people shout "goodbye" and leave.*)

TIM: Fairy Godfather!

FAIRY GODFATHER: Yes, Tim?

TIM: Will you ever come back?

FAIRY GODFATHER: If you ever really need me, Tim, I'll be here! But I think you're going to be *very* busy! (*He exits.*)

SALLY: Tim, were they really here?

TIM: (*Opening a book*) Who?

SALLY: Tim, do you believe they were real?

TIM: (*Looking at her*) Oh, Sally—they were real pretend, of course, just as they said! And that's the realest kind of real there is. Now don't bother me. I'm reading!

THE END

Think About It

1. Explain how Tim felt about reading at the beginning of the play. Which things in the play helped you know this?
2. What were the Fairy Godfather and the book characters trying to make Tim understand?
3. If you wanted to help someone like books, what would you do?
4. Tell about a favorite character from a book that you would like to have as a real pretend friend.
5. Would Judy Blume agree with the Fairy Godfather? Why or why not?

Explore
Do a survey of family members and friends outside your class. Find out who their favorite children's storybook characters are.

Create and Share
Add your survey list to those of others in the class. Find out who the five most popular characters are from your surveys.

A Good Deed, Indeed!

One good deed deserves another.

an old saying

A Thousand Pails of Water

by Ronald Roy

Yukio lived in a fishing village where people fished to make their living. Yukio's father, too, was a fisherman.

"Why do you fish, Father?" Yukio asked. "Suki's father works in the market. He works regular hours and never smells of fish."

"Fishing is all I know," his father answered.

But Yukio did not understand.

Yukio went to his grandfather and asked again, "Why does my father fish?"

"Your father does what he likes to do," his grandfather said. "Let him be, little one, and ask your questions of the sea."

So Yukio went to the sea.

Small creatures scurried from under his feet in the tide pools. Large scavenger birds screamed at him from the sky, "Bring us food!"

Then Yukio saw a whale that had become lodged between some rocks and was left behind when the tide went out.

The large tail flukes beat the sand, helplessly. The eye, as big as Yukio's hand, rolled in fright.

Yukio knew that the whale would not live long out of the sea.

"I will help you, sir," he said.

But how? The whale was huge, like a temple.

Yukio raced to the water's edge. Was the tide coming in or going out? In, he decided, by the way the little fingers of foam climbed higher with each new wave.

The sun was hot on Yukio's back as he stood looking at the whale.

Yukio filled his pail with water and threw it over the great head.

"You are so big and my pail is so small!" he cried. "But I will throw a thousand pails of water over you before I stop."

The second pail went on the head as well, and the third and the fourth. But Yukio knew he must wet every part of the whale or it would die in the sun.

Yukio made many trips to the sea for water, counting as he went. He threw four pails on the body, then four on the tail, and then three on the head.

There was a little shade on one side of the big gray prisoner. Yukio sat there, out of breath, his heart pounding. Then he looked in the whale's eye and remembered his promise.

Yukio went back to the sea and stopped to fill his pail. How many had he filled so far? He had lost count. But he knew he must not stop.

Yukio fell, the precious water spilling from his pail. He cried, and his tears disappeared into the sand.

A wave touched his foot, as if to say, "Get up and carry more water. I am coming, but I am very slow."

Yukio filled his pail over and over. His back hurt, and his arms—but he threw and threw.

He fell again, but this time he did not get up.

Yukio felt himself being lifted.

"You have worked hard, little one. Now let us help."

Yukio's grandfather laid him in the shade of one of the rocks. Yukio watched his grandfather throw his first pail of water and go for another.

"Hurry!" Yukio wanted to scream, for his grandfather was old and walked slowly.

Then Yukio heard the voices. His father and the village people were running toward the sea. They carried pails and buckets and anything that would hold water.

Some of the villagers removed their jackets and soaked them in the sea. These they placed on the whale's burning skin. Soon the whale was wet all over.

Slowly the sea came closer and closer. At last it covered the huge tail. The village people ran back and forth carrying water, shouting to each other. Yukio knew the whale would be saved.

Yukio's father came and stood by him. "Thank you, Father," Yukio said, "for bringing the village people to help."

"You are strong and good," his father said. "But to save a whale many hands must carry the water."

Now the whale was moving with each new wave. Suddenly a great one lifted him free of the rocks. He was still for a moment, then, with a flip of his tail, swam out to sea.

The villagers watched silently, as the whale swam farther and farther from their shore. Then they turned and walked toward the village.

Except for Yukio, who was asleep in the arms of his father.

He had carried a thousand pails of water, and he was tired.

Think About It

1. What does this story tell you about the kind of person Yukio is?
2. Why didn't Yukio go for help right away?
3. What lessons could Yukio learn from saving the whale?
4. Tell how Yukio's family feels about his good deed. Find some words in the story that let you know this.

Create and Share   What do you think the whale might say to Yukio if it were able to talk? Draw a picture of the whale. Put the whale's words in a speech balloon.

Explore   The author of this story, Ronald Roy, used to teach school. Now he uses all of his time to write books for children. Find a book by Ronald Roy and read more of his stories.

GOOD DEEDS

from JATAKA TALES
edited by Nancy DeRoin

Once upon a time in the Kasi country, there lived a rich merchant who secretly buried a fortune in gold beneath his house. Years passed, and the merchant died without ever telling anyone about the secret gold. As time went by, people moved away and the village became empty.

One day, a little mouse came to live in the old house. She soon discovered the gold. But since a mouse cannot use gold, she still had to hunt for her daily food. One morning as she was searching for breakfast, she came upon a stone cutter digging up huge rocks near the village. She thought to herself:

"When I die, the secret of all that gold will die with me. Why not share it with this hardworking young man?" So she took a gold coin in her mouth and brought it to the stone cutter.

The stone cutter was amazed. "Why mother mouse!" he exclaimed, "have you brought this for me?"

The mouse replied, "Yes, it is for you. Perhaps you will share your food with me in return, my son?"

Delighted, the stone cutter took the coin and bought a store of food for himself and shared it with the mouse. When the food was gone, the mouse brought him a second coin, then a third, and so on, day after day. The stone cutter still worked at his trade, and the mouse still lived in the old house, but both were free from hunger.

Then, one day, the little mouse was caught by a cat.

"Oh, don't kill me!" the mouse cried.

"Why not?" asked the cat. "I'm as hungry as I can be, and I really must kill you in order to eat."

"Only wait," the mouse replied. "I promise to bring you meat much tastier than I am, if only you will let me go."

"Mind that you do, then," the hungry cat replied.

So when the stone cutter came that day with food, the mouse had to share it with the cat.

The next day the cat came back. "I'm hungry again, and I am going to eat you," the cat announced.

"But I fed you and you promised to let me go," the mouse said.

"Yes, but that was yesterday," said the cat, "and today is today, and I am hungry again."

The mouse promised the cat more meat and again shared what the stone cutter brought. This went on for several days.

As luck would have it, the mouse was caught by a second cat. She had to buy her life the same way. Now she was sharing her daily food with two cats. She began to grow thin. Noticing this, the stone cutter brought her more food each day. Finally, a third cat caught the mouse. The mouse brought her food also. Now the mouse had to divide her food into four parts—and her own part was very small.

At last, the mouse was nothing but skin and bones. Seeing how his friend looked, the stone cutter asked her if she were sick.

She told him all that had been happening.

"Why did you not tell me this before?" the stone cutter said. "But cheer up, mother, I will help you out of your troubles."

He took a block of pure crystal and polished it with great skill until it was as clear as air. One could look straight through it and not even know it was there. Then he carved out a tiny hole, just big enough for a mouse, and told his friend to crawl inside.

He said to her, "Now, when your cats come for their supper, be sure to tease and insult them."

The mouse waited inside the crystal. Soon, one of the cats came and, seeing nothing strange, demanded her meat.

"Away, you stupid cat!" the little mouse cried. "Why should I feed you? Go home and have kittens!"

The cat could not believe her ears! And since the mouse kept insulting her, the cat finally sprang at her. But instead of capturing the mouse, the cat bumped up against the crystal with such a bang that she fell backward and tumbled away. She was so terrified to see that the mouse was not hurt that she ran away.

Soon, the second cat arrived. "Give me my meat, mouse," he demanded.

"Get it yourself, you lazy good-for-nothing," the mouse answered.

"I'll show you who's lazy." The cat snarled and sprang at the mouse with his fangs bared. Instead of sinking them into the mouse, the cat's fangs broke on the hard crystal. Just like the first cat, the second cat ran away in terror.

When the third cat arrived, the mouse was sleeping inside the crystal with her head between her paws.

"Wake up and get my meat! I'm starved," the cat said.

"Why don't you bring meat for *me* today?" the mouse suggested sweetly. "I'm really rather tired."

"*Tired?*" the angry cat screamed. "You'll soon be dead!" And she sprang at the mouse—only to come up against a solid, but invisible, wall of crystal. The third cat also ran away in blind fear, and none of them ever returned.

The grateful mouse took the stone cutter to the old house and showed him the buried fortune. The two friends, mouse and stone cutter, lived there in friendship until the very end of their lives, for, as the stone cutter said:

One good deed deserves another,
When it comes to friends.
But once you try to freedom buy,
Paying never ends.

Think About It

1. How did the buried gold help both the stone cutter and the mouse?
2. Explain what the stone cutter's poem at the end of the story means.
3. List some words from the story to tell what each of the characters is like.
4. Which good deed is the best good deed in this story? Why?

Explore   Ask family members to help you find examples of good deeds that are written up in the newspaper or included in television or radio news.

Create and Share   Describe in your own words one of these good deed stories you found. Write a short summary and add it to a class bulletin board titled "Good Deeds in the News."

Helping

Agatha Fry, she made a pie,
And Christopher John helped bake it.
Christopher John, he mowed the lawn,
And Agatha Fry helped rake it.
Zachary Zugg took out the rug,
And Jennifer Joy helped shake it,
And Jennifer Joy, she made a toy,
And Zachary Zugg helped break it.

And some kind of help
Is the kind of help
That helping's all about.
And some kind of help
Is the kind of help
We can do without.

—Shel Silverstein
from WHERE THE SIDEWALK ENDS

Quarter for a Haircut

from SOUP & ME
by Robert Newton Peck

"Let me see it," said Soup.

"You just saw it."

"But I just want to see it again."

"Okay," I said.

As we walked along the dusty dirt road toward town, I took the coin from my pocket so Soup could take another squint at it. The afternoon sun turned it shiny.

"Gee," said Soup, "a whole quarter."

"And it's all mine," I said.

"Won't be for long."

"I know.   I got to turn over the whole thing to the barber, Mr. Petty."

"You can't ask him to cut you hair for free," said Soup.

"Reckon I can't."

"You know something, Rob?"

"What?"

"If I was a barber, and you came to my barbershop, I'd cut your hair for free."

"You really would?"

"Sure would," said Soup.

"Then I sure wish you were Mr. Petty."

"Rob . . . today might be your lucky day."

"Today?"

"Yup.   Maybe you won't *have* to give your quarter to the barber."

"Oh yes, I do, Soup.   My mother said I was to go straight to town and not stop until I got to Mr. Petty's.   She didn't seem to care what else I came home with, as long as I left some hair in town."

"Your hair looks okay to me," said Soup.

"It looks okay to me, too.   Like it always does."

"Well, it's kind of long in back."

"So's yours," I said.

Soup said, "Always is by the end of August. Seeing as school starts up again next week, I got a hunch my mother will pack me off to Mr. Petty's as soon as her nose gets a smell of your haircut."

"Probably will," I said.

"Twenty-five pennies," said Soup. "That would trade for a mighty mess of bubble gum."

"Yeah," I said, "it sure would."

"We could buy enough Pink Awful to last us all winter."

I looked at the quarter in my hand. My mind could suddenly see it in Mr. Petty's hand, gone forever.

"It's an honest shame," said Soup.

"What is?"

"Giving up a whole winter's worth of Pink Awful to Mr. Petty. I bet his false teeth couldn't even make a dent in it."

"You're telling me," I said. "And if there was any way around it . . ."

"There is."

"What do you mean, Soup?"

"Rob."

"Yeah?"

"Know what I might be when I grow up?"

"No, what?" For a moment, I thought Soup was changing the subject.

"A barber," said Soup.

Turning the corner into town, we were standing on Main Street. Only a few doors away was Petty's Barbershop. It was the only one in town. It was almost as if Soup could read my thoughts.

"There's the candy store," he nodded in its direction.

"I gotta get a haircut," I said.

"Wouldn't hurt to just look in the window, would it?"

"I don't guess it would," I said, knowing full well that this was a trap, and wanting to step into it with both feet.

As I looked in the window, Soup looked across the street at Mr. Petty's.

"Yes," he said, "someday I'll have my own barbershop."

"Honest?"

"Honest. Already gave my cousin a haircut."

"You did, Soup?"

"For *free*."

That was the magic word—*free*. It rang like a little silver bell.

"Free," repeated Soup. He whispered it.

"Could you cut *mine* for free?" I said.

"You know," he said, "I could."

"Quick," I said, "let's borrow some scissors."

"Let's get the gum first," said Soup.

Tumbling over each other in our excitement, we took a full second to enter the candy store.

"What do *you* want?" asked Mr. Jubert. Soup and I had been in his store on many an earlier shopping spree.

"Bubble gum," said Soup with little hesitation.

"What kind?" asked Mr. Jubert.

"Pink Awful," said Soup, pointing to a tray of goodies.

"How much?" asked old Jubert.

"A quarter's worth," said Soup.

Mr. Jubert had not expected such a big purchase.

"Let me see it," said Mr. Jubert.

"See what?" I said.

"The quarter," he croaked.

My hand shook a bit as I showed him the quarter. The expression on his face did not soften. Without a word, his dirty fingers reached inside. Without looking, without counting, his hand clutched exactly twenty-five pieces. Soup and I both reached for them.

"Not so fast," said Mr. Jubert.

Before I could say even a word, Mr. Jubert's other hand struck like a cobra and closed on my quarter, snatching it from my fingers. I didn't even see it disappear. It just went.

The gum was now mine.

329

Yet somehow I couldn't bring myself to touch it. Neither could Soup. We just stood and stared at the twenty-five pink packages. The brand was Pink Awe. But nobody called it that. Someone had thought of calling it Pink Awful, as it was pink; and to anyone except a kid, tasted awful. Perhaps the nickname came from trying to pry a pink wad from the sole of a shoe. The name stuck as well.

"Anything else?"

"No, thank you." I answered Mr. Jubert.

"Do you have a pair of shears, Mr. Jubert?" Soup asked.

"*Shears?* What for?" Mr. Jubert scowled.

"I want to cut something," said Soup.

"What do you aim to cut?"

"A lock of my hair." I said. "We need it for a reason."

"Go do it outside," said Mr. Jubert.

We hurriedly exited.

Mr. Jubert kept our gum until we returned with his tool. Nobody would call those gigantic shears barbering scissors. They were sure big.

Once outside, it was amazing how fast Soup cut my hair. Any wisp or curl that stuck out got whacked off. Those big shears made such a noise with the bang of their blades. *Clank.* Rang out like a church bell. Down at my feet another ring (of curls) surrounded my blue sneakers.

"Hey, Soup?"

"Yeah." *Clank. Clank.*

"Don't take off too much. Winter's coming."

"It's still August and hot as a hayloft. Oops, I just made a mistake. You gotta hold still." *Clank Clank Clank.*

"What kind of mistake?"

"Well, I sort of went too deep in one spot. Maybe I can sort of even it off." *Clank.*

"How?"

"Just cut a bit here . . ." *Clank* "and over there . . ." *Clank* "so it doesn't show up as bad."

"What doesn't show?"

"Your skin."

"You mean my *scalp?*"

"Yeah." *Clank Clank.* "Oops!"

"What happened?"

"Just another mistake." *Clank Clank Clank.*

"Don't you think you took enough off?"

"Hold still. I'm not taking any more off." *Clank.*

"You're still cutting."

"Not really cutting. Just kind of evening it."

"Do a good job, Soup."

"Don't worry."

I wasn't one to worry much. Except when Soup told me that I didn't have a worry in the world. Only then did my hands start to sweat. I looked at my palms. They were wet. *Clank Clank Clank.*

"Oops," said Soup.

"Another mistake?"

"Sort of. But it's small. No one will ever notice because it's right next to one of the big . . ."

"One of the big *what?*"

"Big mistakes." *Clank.* "There, I'm all done."

"You sure put a lot of hair down my neck. How do I look?"

Without waiting to hear Soup's reply, I turned to find my reflection in the candy store window. I sure did look different. No denying I'd had a haircut. It didn't look really bad. Then again, you wouldn't say it looked real good either. Twisting away from the glass, I saw Soup down on his knees. Using his hands, he swept up my cut-off hair and then stood up, stuffing my hair into his pocket.

"Let's go," said Soup.

Returning the shears to the counter of the candy store, we started to pick up the gum. Old Jubert had his back to us as we walked in. Turning, he saw us. Then he saw *me!* He head bobbed forward like a turkey and his mouth popped open. It was the first time I'd ever seen Mr. Jubert's face change its look. He darn near smiled.

Soup and I chewed gum all the way home. We'd chew a sheet of Pink Awful, pop some bubbles with it, and then when all the flavor was gone, we'd spit a pink cud into the dust of the road and help ourselves to fresh. Sure was fun.

"Stop," ordered Soup.

I stopped—chewing and walking.

"Rob," he said, "you're my pal. Right?"

"Yeah, I'm your pal."

"So I can't let your mother and your Aunt Carrie see you the way you are. What's the first thing those two will do when you get back?"

"They'll inspect my haircut."

Soup nodded. "That's why we got to do a patch job."

"A patch job? Like on a *tire?*"

"Sort of." Soup spat out his gum, this time into his hand. He rubbed it on my head, around and around, sometimes in small circles and then in bigger ones.

"How come you're putting bubble gum in my hair, Soup?"

"So the hair will stick."

"What hair?"

Soup reached into his pocket and came up with a handful. "*This* hair."

He began to put back hair on the places he'd rubbed on the gum.

"Suppose it comes off," I said.

"Pink Awful *never* comes off," said Soup.

But not even Soup could be right all the time. At the hands of my mother, the hair and most of the Pink Awful did come off when my head was held under the pump.

Think About It

1. What do the poem "Helping" and the story "Quarter for a Haircut" show about some kinds of help?
2. Why does Rob let Soup cut his hair?
3. At what point in the story did you know that Rob was headed for trouble?
4. Do you think Soup meant to get his friend in trouble? Why or why not?
5. Explain what you think Rob will do the next time Soup offers to help.

Create and Share   Write what you think Rob says to his mother to explain his haircut. Write what his mother says to him!

Explore   Robert Newton Peck has written other books about Soup and Rob. Find one of these to read. Or read another story about friends who help each other.

The Sunflower Garden

by Janice May Udry

Pipsa was a little Algonkian Indian girl who lived in the eastern part of our country. She had five brothers but no sister. All the brothers except one were older than Pipsa. He was still a baby.

Pipsa's father was proud of how well her brothers could swim. He didn't notice how well Pipsa took care of her baby brother.

Her father was proud of how well her brothers caught fish. He didn't notice how many berries Pipsa picked.

Her father was proud of how far out into the river her brothers could throw stones. He didn't notice how much wood Pipsa gathered for the fires.

Her father was proud of the way her brothers had learned to trap rabbits and birds. He didn't notice the baskets Pipsa had made.

Her father was proud of the first bows made by her brothers. He didn't notice that now Pipsa helped her mother make their clothes from deerskin.

Pipsa's father taught his sons to do the things he could do, and he often praised them. He never thought of praising a little girl.

But Pipsa's mother was proud of her and sometimes said, "Well done, my little Pipsa!"

Every spring, after the redbud bloomed, Pipsa helped her mother plant corn and beans and squash. How her brothers loved to eat! They seldom helped with the planting or the hoeing, however.

Pipsa's oldest brother was now allowed to take part in the Corn Dance, which was the Indian way of asking the Great Spirit for a good corn crop.

This year, Pipsa was eager for planting time to come. All winter she had been saving some special seeds in her private little birch-bark box. These were sunflower seeds she had gathered in the fall when her family had visited another village. There Pipsa had seen the big sunflowers growing, and she had tasted the delicious cakes that had been made from the seeds. One of the girls in the village had helped her gather leftover seeds. She told Pipsa that the seeds also made wonderful oil for the hair.

Now that spring was here, Pipsa planned to have a sunflower garden. No one in Pipsa's village had ever grown sunflowers. All of the work of growing them would have to be done by Pipsa herself, because her mother had all the work she could manage to do in the big corn and bean field.

While Pipsa's brothers swam and fished and practiced with their bows and arrows, Pipsa and her mother planted and hoed the vegetables. Now that Gray Squirrel, the baby brother, was over a year old, he was no longer fastened to his cradle board, and he toddled about close to his mother and sister.

The days grew warmer and warmer. Almost the only time Pipsa could work in her sunflower patch was after supper. Since the days were longer, it was light enough for her to work then. She usually had to take Gray Squirrel with her and watch that he didn't wander away into the woods.

First, Pipsa scraped away the dead leaves, the old weeds and the sticks. Then she dug and chopped the ground with a hoe and broke up all the dirt clods. She planted the sunflower seeds on an evening when she had heard her father say it would rain before morning. As she looked down at the bare, flat ground where she had planted the seeds, she wondered if the seeds were really any good. Had she planted them right? Would they grow? Pipsa waited and watched for a sign of green.

Finally, after twelve days, the first green shoot appeared. In the next week Pipsa's garden became full of little plants reaching for the sun.

Every evening she chopped down any weed that had dared to invade the baby plants during the day. When the ground was dry, she watched the sky for rain clouds.

It was a good growing summer. By July, the great sunflower heads were heavy with seeds, and it would soon be time to pick them and shake out the seeds for making cakes and oil. Pipsa had to watch Gray Squirrel constantly because he wanted to play with the sunflower heads, and he kept trying to pull them down.

The other mothers and children often came to see and admire Pipsa's big bright flowers. One of the plants was truly a giant sunflower "tree," twice as tall as Pipsa.

As the seeds ripened, Pipsa found that some other creatures loved the sunflowers too.

"The birds and the mice are eating all my seeds," Pipsa told her mother sadly. She spent as much time as she could guarding the sunflowers and shooing the birds.

One evening when Pipsa was chopping weeds away from the plants and Gray Squirrel was crawling around the big leaves, Pipsa suddenly heard something frightening. She stopped and looked quickly for her baby brother. Pipsa heard a rattlesnake!

She saw the coiled creature—the biggest snake she had ever seen! It was lying in the grass waiting for the mice that came for the seeds. Now her little brother had disturbed it. The baby didn't see the snake or know what the sound meant. Pipsa put her hand to her mouth and then, grasping the hoe, she crept swiftly and silently toward the snake. She must kill it before it bit her brother. She had never been so afraid in all her life. What if she missed? What if she only angered the snake?

With all the force she had, Pipsa whacked downward, aiming at the back of the snake's head with the hoe. Without stopping to see if she had killed it, she hit again and again. Very frightened by this time, little Gray Squirrel scrambled to his feet.

"Run, little brother, run!" cried Pipsa.

Gray Squirrel ran crying to his mother.

In a few minutes, Pipsa's mother and father and brothers came running. Gray Squirrel was still crying in his mother's arms.

Pipsa felt so weak that she had to sit down. But beside her was the dead snake. Her brothers were amazed at the size of it. They praised Pipsa for her courage, and for the first time Pipsa's father bent over her and said, "Well done, my little daughter. You are a brave child."

Pipsa was so overcome by the fright of killing the snake that tears came to her eyes. But she fought them back. She didn't want to spoil this moment by crying!

Her father looked around him at the sunflower garden. It was the first time he had been there.

"What are these?" he asked her, puzzled.

"They are sunflowers, Father," she told him.

"What are they for?"

Pipsa told her father that soon they would have good little cakes from the seeds—if she could keep the birds and mice away long enough. And she told him how they could make hair oil.

Pipsa's father asked her how soon they could have these things. He touched the big sunflower heads with great interest. And then he looked again at Pipsa almost as if he had never really seen her before.

He put his big hand on her head. "I am proud of you," he said.

The next day, her father told her brothers to take turns helping Pipsa guard the sunflowers until it was time to gather the seeds.

Finally, when Pipsa said that the seeds were ripe, almost everyone came to watch her gather them.

They all followed Pipsa and her family back to their home, and they watched Pipsa pound the seeds into little cakes. She gave everyone a taste. They smiled and exclaimed at the good flavor. Pipsa told them how to make oil for more beautiful hair. She gave everyone some of the seeds so that the following spring everyone in the village could grow sunflowers.

The whole village spoke proudly of the little girl who had brought a new plant and new ideas to her people. They called her the "Sunflower Girl."

As the years went by, the Indians in Pipsa's village grew more and more sunflowers, and they never forgot to give special honor to Pipsa even after she was grown and had a little girl of her own. The people often told Pipsa's little girl how her mother had grown the first sunflowers there and had given seeds to the rest of the village.

And Pipsa's brother, Gray Squirrel, never forgot that, when he was very small, she had saved his life.

Think About It

1. Why do you think Pipsa's father treated her the way he did at the beginning of the story?
2. How did Pipsa's deeds help people?
3. How do you think Pipsa felt when her father said that he was proud of her?
4. Who do you think gets the most from a good deed—the person who gives or the person who receives? Use the stories you have read to explain what you think.

Create and Share   Think about a time when you did something special and someone was proud of you. Write about what you did and how you felt. Put your story on the bulletin board.

Explore   Search for another story that you feel describes A GOOD DEED, INDEED! Retell the story to the class.

Glossary

Full pronunciation key* The pronunciation of each word is shown just after the word, in this way: **ab·bre·vi·ate** (ə brē′vē āt).

The letters and signs used are pronounced as in the words below.

The mark ′ is placed after a syllable with a primary or heavy accent, as in the example above.

The mark ′ after a syllable shows a secondary or lighter accent as in **ab·bre·vi·a·tion** (ə brē′vē ā′shən).

a	hat, cap	**k**	kind, seek	**₮H**	then, smooth
ā	age, face	**l**	land, coal	**u**	cup, butter
ä	father, far	**m**	me, am	**u̇**	full, put
b	bad, rob	**n**	no, in	**ü**	rule, move
ch	child, much	**ng**	long, bring		
d	did, red	**o**	hot, rock	**v**	very, save
e	let, best	**ō**	open, go	**w**	will, women
ē	equal, be	**ô**	order, all	**y**	young, yet
ėr	term, learn	**oi**	oil, voice	**z**	zero, breeze
f	fat, if	**ou**	house, out	**zh**	measure, seizure
g	go, bag	**p**	paper, cup	**ə**	represents:
h	he, how	**r**	run, try		*a* in about
i	it, pin	**s**	say, yes		*e* in taken
ī	ice, five	**sh**	she, rush		*i* in pencil
j	jam, enjoy	**t**	tell, it		*o* in lemon
		th	thin, both		*u* in circus

*Pronunciation Key and respellings are from *Scott, Foresman Intermediate Dictionary* by E. L. Thorndike and Clarence L. Barnhart. Copyright © 1983 by Scott, Foresman and Co. Reprinted by permission.

a·ban·doned (ə ban′dənd) left behind; left alone; deserted (No one had lived in the *abandoned* house for years.)

ab·bre·vi·a·tion (ə brē′ vē ā′shən) a short way to write a word or group of words ("U.S.A." is the *abbreviation* for "United States of America.")

ac·count (ə kount′) money in a bank; a record of money saved (I have an *account* at First Bank.)

ac·tu·al (ak′ chü əl) real; true (I told my mother the *actual* story of how I broke my glasses.)

ad·mire (ad mīr′) to think something is good or pleasant (Carol *admired* the picture that Harry drew.) **admired, admiring**

aer·o·gramme (er′ə gram) writing paper that folds to make an envelope with postage printed on it

al·ley (al′ē) a narrow street between buildings

an·nounce (ə nouns′) to say out loud; to tell about something (The principal *announced* the winners of the writing contest.)

anx·ious (angk′shəs) worried about something (Irene was *anxious* about the sick dog.)

a·pol·o·gize (ə pol′ə jīz) to say you are sorry **apologized, apologizing**

ar·e·a (er′ē ə) an amount of space (They searched the *area* carefully for the lost watch.)

ar·gue (är′gyü) to talk in an angry way; to fight with words (We sometimes *argue* about who has the best bike.) **argued, arguing**

at·tach (ə tach′) to fasten; to connect (You can *attach* that card to the package with a piece of tape.)

av·er·age (av′ər ij) regular; usual; not the most or the least (Karla is an *average* soccer player. She plays well, but she isn't the best player on the team.)

awe·some (ô′səm) amazing; wonderful (The sight of the snow-covered mountains was *awesome*.)

B

bal·loon·ist (bə lü′nist) a person who flies a hot-air balloon

bam·boo (bam bü′) a kind of woodlike grass that is very tall and stiff (My grandfather's fishing rod was made of *bamboo*.)

bar·ber (bär′bər) a person who cuts hair (I asked the *barber* to cut my hair short for summer.)

bar·ber·ing (bär′bər ing) the act of cutting hair

bar·ber·shop (bär′bər shop′) a place to get a haircut

birch·bark (bėrch′bärk′) the bark of a birch tree

both·er (boᴛʜ′ər) to trouble someone or cause problems; to annoy (Don't *bother* Mom when she gets home from work.)

bruised (brüzd) hurt; black and blue as a result of being hurt (His *bruised* knee hurt.)

C

cap·ture (kap′chər) to catch and keep (We used a trap to *capture* the mouse.) **captured, capturing**

chim·ney (chim′nē) a tall pipe or tube that carries smoke away from a fire

clasp (klasp) to grip firmly with the hand

coax (kōks) to talk someone into doing something by using nice words (Sheila *coaxed* Dan into lending her his bike.)

com·mand (kə mand′) to give an order (I *command* you to pick up the trash.)

---

a hat / ā age / ä far / e let / ē equal / ėr term / i it / ī ice / o hot / ō open / ô order / oi oil / ou out / u cup /
 u̇ put / ü rule / ch child / ng long / sh she / th thin / ᴛʜ then / zh measure / ə a in about, e in taken,
i in pencil, o in lemon, u in circus

con·fide (kən fīd′) to tell a secret (I will *confide* in you, but please don't tell anyone else.) **confided, confiding**

con·fus·ing (kən fyü′zing) hard to understand (The directions for this game are too *confusing*.)

con·fu·sion (kən fyü′zhən) something that is all mixed up; the state of being all mixed up (In the *confusion* after the party, I put on someone else's jacket.)

con·stant·ly (kon′stənt lē) all the time; without stopping (Her radio plays *constantly*.)

con·tin·ue (kən tin′yü) to keep on without stopping (If you *continue* to run every day, your legs will get strong.) **continued, continuing**

con·vince (kən vins′) to make someone sure of something; to make someone believe (Carlos *convinced* me that there was enough popcorn for everybody.) **convinced, convincing**

cour·age (kėr′ij) bravery (It took a lot of *courage* to cross the country in a covered wagon.)

crea·ture (krē′chər) a living person or animal (I heard a small *creature* moving through the leaves.)

cru·el (krü′əl) causing pain or hurt; unkind; mean (The *cruel* bully twisted my arm.)

crys·tal (kris′tl) a clear, shiny rock that looks like glass

cur·i·os·i·ty (kyùr′ ē os′ə tē) interest; desire to know (Her *curiosity* made her ask a lot of questions.)

cur·tain (kėrt′n) **1.** cloth hung over a window (Open the *curtain* and let the sun shine in.) **2.** cloth that hangs in front of a stage (When the *curtain* rises, the play will begin.)

cus·tom (kus′təm) the regular way of doing things (It is a *custom* in our family to open birthday presents at breakfast time.)

cy·clone (sī'klōn) a very strong windstorm (The *cyclone* knocked trees over.)

D

dai·ly (dā'lē) every day (I brush my teeth three times *daily*.)

dare (der) to ask someone to do something, usually something scary or difficult (I *dare* you to jump across the brook.) **dared, daring**

de·ci·sion (di sizh'ən) a choice (We made a *decision* to move to a new town.)

de·clare (di kler') to say out loud; to say strongly (Dad *declared* that Tom had to clean his room.) **declared, declaring**

def·i·nite·ly (def'ə nit lē) certainly; surely; without a doubt (We will *definitely* go swimming today.)

de·li·cious (di lish'əs) good-tasting (Dad prepared a *delicious* meal for us.)

dense (dens) thick; close together (Horses that stay outdoors grow long, *dense* coats in cold weather.) **denser, densest**

de·ny (di nī') to say that something isn't true (If you say I am lazy, I will *deny* it.) **denied, denying**

de·pend (di pend') to rely on; to need something (Grandmother and grandfather *depend* on us to mow their lawn.)

de·scrip·tive (di skrip'tiv) telling what something is like; describing something ("Shaggy" is a *descriptive* name for a dog with long hair.)

des·per·ate (des'pər it) wanting something badly when there is not much hope (After the last bus passed, I was *desperate* to get home.)

des·per·ate·ly (des'pər it lē) in a way that shows great fear or loss of hope (I tried *desperately* to get the bus driver's attention.)

---

a hat / ā age / ä far / e let / ē equal / ėr term / i it / ī ice / o hot / ō open / ô order / oi oil / ou out / u cup / ů put / ü rule / ch child / ng long / sh she / th thin / ᴛʜ then / zh measure / ə a in about, e in taken, i in pencil, o in lemon, u in circus

des·sert (di zėrt′) food served at the end of a meal, often something sweet

di·a·per (dī′ə pər) a soft piece of cloth or other material worn by a baby as underpants

di·ar·y (dī′ər ē) a book to write in, usually to say what happens each day (Every night I write the best thing that happened that day in my *diary*.) *pl.* **diaries**

dis·ap·point·ment (dis′ ə point′mənt) **1.** the feeling you have when you don't get what you want (*Disappointment* filled me when I opened the gift.) **2.** something that is not what you want (The change in our vacation plans was a big *disappointment*.)

dis·gust·ing (dis gus′ting) awful; yucky (The dirty dishes were a *disgusting* mess.)

dis·o·bey (dis′ ə bā′) not to do as you are told; to break the rules

dis·turb (dis tėrb′) to interrupt, bother, or upset (Don't *disturb* me when I am studying.)

down·pour (doun′pôr′) a heavy rainstorm

down·ward (doun′wərd) toward the ground; toward the bottom (The diver swam *downward* to the ocean floor.)

driv·en (driv′ən) made to go somewhere or do something (The cows were *driven* into the field.)

E

east·ern (ē′stərn) toward the east; from the east; in the east (Aunt Louise lives in *eastern* Maryland.)

en·trance (en′trəns) a way in (People crowded around the *entrance* to the store.)

es·cape (e skāp′) to get away from someone or some place **escaped, escaping**

e·vil (ē′vəl) bad; wrong; wicked (The scary woman in the dark cape looked *evil*.)

ex·hib·it (eg zib′it) a show or display (The art teacher made an *exhibit* of our best paintings.)

ex·it (eg′zit *or* ek′sit) the way out (We go to the *exit* quickly during a fire drill.)

ex·pect (ek spekt′) to think something will happen; to be ready (I missed the ball because I didn't *expect* you to throw it so fast.)

ex·pen·sive (ek spen′siv) costing a lot of money (The shoes I want are too *expensive*.)

ex·pres·sion (ek spresh′ən) a look on someone's face (She had a happy *expression* when she heard who was the winner.)

ex·ten·ded (ek sten′dəd) stretched out (Jeff put the orange in Carol's *extended* hand.)

F

faint (fānt) weak; not clear (Only a *faint* light came from the small candle.) **fainter, faintest**

fes·ti·val (fes′tə vəl) a special day to celebrate; a celebration (We watched the skating races at the winter *festival*.)

fierce (firs) wild; scary (She gave a *fierce* cry.)

flood (flud) **1.** to cover, usually with water or some other liquid (Water from the hose *flooded* the garden.) **2.** a great amount of water that covers an area that is usually dry (The *flood* from the river covered our backyard.)

fluke (flük) one of the flat parts of a whale's tail

force (fôrs) strength; power (She used *force* to move the rock.)

for·tune (fôr′chən) **1.** treasure; riches (We found a *fortune* in old coins in the attic.) **2.** luck (Good *fortune* kept us safe on the trip.)

---

a hat / ā age / ä far / e let / ē equal / ėr term / i it / ī ice / o hot / ō open / ô order / oi oil / ou out / u cup / u̇ put / ü rule / ch child / ng long / sh she / th thin / ŦH then / zh measure / ə a in about, e in taken, i in pencil, o in lemon, u in circus

fur·ni·ture (fėr′nə chər) the things needed in a house, such as tables, chairs, and beds

G

gar·bage (gär′bij) scraps of food that are thrown away

gar·lic (gär′lik) a strong-tasting, onionlike plant used in cooking

gen·u·ine (jen′yü ən) true; real (She has a ring with a *genuine* diamond.)

gi·gan·tic (jī gan′tik) very large; huge (The *gigantic* pizza was big enough for the whole family.)

gov·ern·ment (guv′ərn mənt) **1.** the people who run a country (The *government* makes rules and collects taxes.) **2.** the way a country is run (Different countries have different kinds of *government*.)

gro·cer·ies (grō′sər ēz) food and other things bought at a store for use in a home

guard (gärd) **1.** to protect; to keep safe (The police officer *guarded* the children as they crossed the street.) **2.** a person who protects something (The museum *guard* would not let anyone touch the pictures.)

guest (gest) a visitor (Yesterday, Joe's father was a *guest* in our classroom.)

H

har·vest (här′vist) **1.** the picking of plants for food (The *harvest* of corn was good this year.) **2.** to cut down plants for food; to pick fruit and vegetables (We *harvest* most of the crops in the fall.)

haz·ard (haz′ərd) a danger (Thin ice is a *hazard* for skaters.)

hes·i·tate (hez′ə tāt) to pause; to wait before starting (I sometimes *hesitate* before I jump into a cold lake.) **hesitated, hesitating**

hock·ey (hok′ē) **1.** a game played by skaters on ice, with sticks and a flat rubber circle called a puck **2.** a game played in a field, with sticks and a ball

hon·or·a·ble (on′ər ə bəl) **1.** noble; good (We were glad that such an *honorable* person would visit us.) **2.** honest

hon·ored (on′ərd) respected; well liked

hur·ri·cane (hėr′ə kān) a storm with strong winds and a lot of rain

I

im·me·di·ate·ly (i mē′dē it lē) at once; right away (He does his homework *immediately* after supper.)

im·prove (im prüv′) to get better (Your playing will *improve* if you practice.) **improved, improving**

in·crease (in krēs′) to make larger or greater (Some people would like to *increase* the time children spend in school each year.)

in·spect (in spekt′) to look at closely; to check up on (They *inspect* all the playground equipment every year to be sure that it is safe.)

in·sult (in sult′) to say unkind and untrue things to someone (Don't *insult* him by calling him silly.)

in·vade (in vād′) to break in; to take over (Ants *invaded* the picnic basket.) **invaded, invading**

in·vi·ta·tion (in′və tā′shən) the act of asking someone to go somewhere or do something (I sent her an *invitation* to my party.)

---

a hat / ā age / ä far / e let / ē equal / ėr term / i it / ī ice / o hot / ō open / ô order / oi oil / ou out / u cup / u̇ put / ü rule / ch child / ng long / sh she / th thin / ᴛʜ then / zh measure / ə a in about, e in taken, i in pencil, o in lemon, u in circus

in·vite (in vīt′) to ask someone nicely to go someplace or do something (Let's *invite* them to go to the movies with us.) **invited, inviting**

i·ron (ī′ərn) a kind of metal

J

juice (jüs) liquid squeezed from a fruit or vegetable

jun·ior (jü′nyər) having the same name as your father (John Jones's son is called John Jones, *Junior.*)

L

lan·guage (lang′gwij) spoken or written words (Do you know anyone who can speak the Spanish *language?*)

leop·ard (lep′ərd) a large, wild member of the cat family, found in Africa and Asia

lodged (lojd) stuck (A tiny piece of popcorn is *lodged* between two of my teeth.)

lov·a·ble (luv′ə bəl) likable; able to be loved (My baby brother is very *lovable* when he smiles.)

M

ma·gi·cian (mə jish′ən) a person who does tricks; someone who can make things happen by using secret ways and saying special words (When the *magician* said a magic word, the rabbit appeared and the scarf disappeared.)

mag·net (mag′nit) a piece of iron or steel that draws other pieces of iron or steel toward it

mam·mal (mam′əl) an animal that feeds its babies with milk (Cows, whales, and mice are all *mammals.*)

mar·a·thon (mar′ə thon) **1.** a running race just a little more than 26 miles long **2.** any very long race or event (Each student will try to read many books during the reading *marathon*.)

mea·sles (mē′zəlz) a sickness that causes a red rash on the skin

mem·o·rize (mem′ə rīz′) to learn by heart (You will have to *memorize* the steps for the dance.) **memorized, memorizing**

men·u (men′yü) a list of things to eat (Hot dogs were not on the *menu*, so I ordered chicken instead.)

mer·chant (mėr′chənt) a person who sells something (The fish *merchant* sold Grandmother some flounder.)

mes·sen·ger (mes′n jər) one who is sent to tell something or deliver something (The *messenger* took a note to the office.)

mill·er (mil′ər) a person who grinds grain into flour

mis·er·a·ble (miz′ər ə bəl) feeling awful; unhappy (Henry was *miserable* when he had a bad cold.)

moun·tain·ous (moun′tə nəs) having many mountains (The explorers climbed for weeks in the *mountainous* country.)

mourn (môrn) to feel sad because someone has died or something is lost

N

nat·ur·al·ly (nach′ər ə lē) in a normal way; of course (I *naturally* thought you would enjoy the party.)

neck·lace (nek′lis) a piece of jewelry worn around the neck

---

a hat / **ā** age / **ä** far / **e** let / **ē** equal / **ėr** term / **i** it / **ī** ice / **o** hot / **ō** open / **ô** order / **oi** oil / **ou** out / **u** cup / **u̇** put / **ü** rule / **ch** child / **ng** long / **sh** she / **th** thin / **ŦH** then / **zh** measure / ə *a* in about, *e* in taken, *i* in pencil, *o* in lemon, *u* in circus

nei·ther (nē′ͭHər) not either one
(*Neither* the boys nor the girls
were noisy in class today.)

noc·tur·nal (nok tėr′nl) active at
night and sleeping during the
day (Bats are *nocturnal*
animals.)

O

oc·cu·pa·tion (ok′yə pā′shən) a
job; a kind of work (Do you
ever wonder what *occupation*
you will choose when you are
grown up?)

old-fash·ioned (ōld′ fash′ənd)
not modern; old in style or in
way of doing things (We wore
old-fashioned clothing in the play
about the pioneers.)

om·e·let (om′lit) a food made of
beaten eggs. It is fried in a pan
or baked in the oven. (*Omelets*
are good for breakfast.)

op·e·ra·tor (op′ə rā′tər) a person
who runs a piece of equipment
(The computer *operator* found
the answers to the math
problems quickly.)

or·di·nar·y (ôrd′n er′ē) normal;
usual (It was an *ordinary* sort of
watch.)

o·ver·due (ō′vər dü′) late (The
train is an hour *overdue*.)

pan·da (pan′də) a rare black and
white bearlike animal that
comes from China

pas·sen·ger (pas′n jər) someone
who rides in a car, bus, plane,
boat, or train

pas·ture (pas′chər) grassy land
that sheep, cows, or horses
can feed on

pat·i·o (pat′ē ō) a place on
ground level that is used for
sitting outdoors (We have a
patio outside our door.)

per·son·al (pėr′sə nəl) private;
belonging to one person

361

pi·an·o (pē an′ō) a large musical instrument played by pressing keys on the outside to make hammers hit strings on the inside

pleas·ant·ly (plez′nt lē) in a pleasing way; nicely

po·si·tion (pə zish′ən) a way of standing or being placed (The blocks might fall over if you leave them in that *position*.)

pos·sess (pə zes′) to have or own (Maria *possesses* the most wonderful kite.)

pos·si·bil·i·ty (pos′ ə bil′ə tē) something that could happen (Sunshine is a *possibility* for the weekend.) *pl.* **possibilities**

post·age (pō′stij) stamps put on a letter or package to pay for sending it by mail

po·ta·to (pə tā′tō) a vegetable that grows underground *pl.* **potatoes**

pour (pôr) **1.** to make something flow smoothly (You *pour* the milk while I make the sandwiches.) **2.** to rain hard (Take a raincoat. It is going to *pour* this afternoon.)

pre·cious (presh′əs) very special; much loved (That toy train is *precious* to Charlie because it belonged to his grandfather.)

pre·dic·tion (pri dik′shən) something that someone says will happen in the future (The coach was right in her *prediction* of who would win the game.)

pri·vate (prī′vit) not for everyone; just for one person or a special group (Our *private* club met in my yard.)

pro·pane (prō′pān) a kind of gas used for heat and light (When we go camping, we cook on a stove that burns *propane*.)

a hat / ā age / ä far / e let / ē equal / ėr term / i it / ī ice / o hot / ō open / ô order / oi oil / ou out / u cup / ů put / ü rule / ch child / ng long / sh she / th thin / ₮ʜ then / zh measure / ə a in about, e in taken, i in pencil, o in lemon, u in circus

pu·pil (pyü′pəl) **1.** a student (Every *pupil* in the class will get a new book.) **2.** the dark center part of the eye (The *pupil* gets smaller in bright light.)

pur·chase (pėr′chəs) **1.** something that is bought (I carried my *purchase* home in a bag.) **2.** to buy (I will *purchase* a new book tomorrow.) **purchased, purchasing**

R

rap·id·ly (rap′id lē) quickly; at a fast rate (He was hungry and ate the sandwich *rapidly*.)

re·ceive (ri sēv′) to get something (I *receive* a book from my aunt every year.) **received, receiving**

re·serve (ri zėrv′) **1.** a place where something can be safe (We saw moose and deer at the wild animal *reserve*.) **2.** to save; to put away to use later (*Reserve* some food for after the game.) **reserved, reserving**

re·sist (ri zist′) to keep from doing (I couldn't *resist* taking one more pancake.)

re·tire·ment (ri tīr′mənt) the time after a person has stopped working at a job, usually because of age (Grandpa likes *retirement* because now he has time for his garden.)

re·ward (ri wôrd′) **1.** a gift given in return for some special job or action (As a *reward* for taking care of her cat, Mrs. Harvey gave Carlos tickets to the baseball game.) **2.** to give something to a person because he or she does something (I will *reward* you for finding the money I lost.)

rhyme (rīm) **1.** to end with the same sound ("Pan" and "fan" *rhyme*.) **2.** a word that has the same sound at the end as another word ("Word" is a *rhyme* for "bird.")

ri·dic·u·lous (ri dik′yə ləs) foolish; silly (Their *ridiculous* looks made us laugh.)

S

scav·en·ger (skav′ən jər) an animal that eats plants or animals that are rotting

scheme (skēm) **1.** a plan for action (Rick has a *scheme* for making a fort in the barn.) **2.** to make a plan (He will *scheme* all night until he figures out a way to escape.) **schemed, scheming**

serv·ice (sėr′vis) a helpful act (By cleaning the sidewalks, the boy scouts performed a *service* for the town.)

si·lent (sī′lənt) quiet; still (The teacher asked us to be *silent* while she read.)

silk·en (sil′kən) **1.** made of silk (The king wore a *silken* robe.) **2.** very smooth like silk (The princess combed her *silken* hair.)

sin·cere·ly (sin sir′lē) honestly; with true feelings (I am *sincerely* sorry.)

sol·dier (sōl′jər) a man or woman in an army

sol·id (sol′id) **1.** hard (He gave the ball a *solid* hit.) **2.** not hollow (All I saw was *solid* rock, with no caves.)

soup (süp) food made with water and such things as meat and vegetables (I like chicken *soup* with rice.)

south·west·ern (south′wes′tərn) in the southwest part (The *southwestern* part of a map is usually in the bottom left corner.)

starved (stärvd) very hungry (We all felt *starved* because dinner was late.)

state·ment (stāt mənt) something that is said (The president made a *statement* on television.)

stom·ach (stum′ək) the part of the body where food goes when you swallow it; the middle part of the body

stom·ach·ache (stum′ək āk′) a pain in the stomach

---

a hat / ā age / ä far / e let / ē equal / ėr term / i it / ī ice / o hot / ō open / ô order / oi oil / ou out / u cup / ù put / ü rule / ch child / ng long / sh she / th thin / ₮H then / zh measure / ə a in about, e in taken, i in pencil, o in lemon, u in circus

sur·name (sėr′nām′) last name or family name (Alice Brown's *surname* is Brown.)

sur·vive (sər vīv′) to keep on living (They didn't think she could *survive* after being so sick.) **survived, surviving**

sym·bol (sim′bəl) a picture or object that stands for something else (A blue line on a map can be a *symbol* for a river.)

T

tax·i (tak′sē) a car that is used to give rides for pay (We rode in a *taxi* to the hotel.)

term (tėrm) a word or group of words connected with a special subject ("Pick your own adventure story" is a *term* for a story in which the reader chooses what will happen next.)

ter·ri·fied (ter′ə fīd) very frightened (The first time I climbed the rope, I was *terrified* that I would fall.)

tire·some (tīr′səm) boring; not interesting (The *tiresome* song repeated the same words over and over.)

to·tal·ly (tō′tl ē) completely (I was *totally* wet after I fell in the brook.)

V

va·ca·tion (vā kā′shən) time away from school or work (I spent most of my summer *vacation* camping.)

val·ley (val′ē) a low place between mountains or hills

vent (vent) an opening; an outlet (A *vent* at the top of the tent let the smoke out.)

verse (vėrs) short poem; part of a poem or song

vic·tor·y (vik′tər ē) the winning of a game or fight (One more soccer *victory* and we will win the prize for our school.) *pl.* **victories**

W

whirl (hwėrl) **1.** to make a thing spin around (She *whirled* the scarf above her head.) **2.** to spin around (The children *whirled* around until they got dizzy.)

wit·ness (wit′nis) someone who sees something happen (The police found a *witness* who had seen the accident.) *pl.* **witnesses**

wom·an (wùm′ən) a lady; a grown-up female (That *woman* is my aunt.)

word proc·ess·or (wėrd′ pros′əs ər) a computer used for writing (Lee used the *word processor* to type a letter.)

a hat / **ā** age / **ä** far / **e** let / **ē** equal / **ėr** term / **i** it / **ī** ice / **o** hot / **ō** open / **ô** order / **oi** oil / **ou** out / **u** cup /
ù put / **ü** rule / **ch** child / **ng** long / **sh** she / **th** thin / ᴛʜ then / **zh** measure / ə *a* in about, *e* in taken,
i in pencil, *o* in lemon, *u* in circus

366

Cover/Cluster Openers   Design: Studio Goodwin-Sturges. **Illustration:** Jerry Pinkney. **Calligraphy:** Colleen.

Editorial   Book Editor: Michael P. Gibbons. **Senior Editor:** Susan D. Paro. **Editorial Services:** Marianna Frew Palmer, K. Kirschbaum Harvie. **Permissions Editor:** Dorothy Burns McLeod.
Design   Series: Leslie Dews. **Book:** Joan Paley, Judy Sue Goodwin-Sturges.
Production   Mary Hunter.

Illustration   **10–11:** Tony Ross. **13–26:** Bert Dodson. **28–36:** Enzo Gianinni. **38–50:** Ron Barrett, copyright © 1978, from *Cloudy With A Chance of Meatballs*, with permission. **54–62:** Gavin Bishop. **92–100:** Beverley Gooding, copyright © 1985, from *Once There Were No Pandas*, with permission. **113–121:** Kees de Kiefte. **136–138:** Mary MacLaren. **142–148:** Carolyn Croll. **150–158:** Jamie Hogan. **160–163:** Bernard Waber, copyright © 1971, from *My Diary*, with permission. **164–172:** Tony Ross. **176–187:** Chris Van Allsburg, copyright © 1979, from *The Garden of Abdul Gasazi*, with permission. **188–203:** Winslow Pinney Pels. **204–206:** laliberte. **210–218:** Blair Lent, copyright © 1968, from *Tikki Tikki Tembo,* with permission. **221–227:** Slug Signorino. **230–244:** Nancy Wiley. **246–258:** Gail Owens. **262–275:** Alan Tiegreen. **276–278:** Mary MacLaren. **279–286:** Irene Trivas, copyright © 1984, from *The Pain and the Great One*, with permission. **288–302:** Sharlene Collicott. **306–312:** Dan Clifford. **314–320:** Mary Azarian. **323–336:** Fred Lynch. **338–348:** Dan Clifford. **351–366:** Cyndy Patrick.

Photography   **64–74:** Photos by © A. Lamorisse used by permission of Unwin Hyman Ltd., London. **76:** North Wind Pictures. **77:** Bettmann Archive. **78:** *l,* David F. Hughes (Picture Cube); *r,* Jennifer D. Cogswell (Picture Cube). **79:** *l,* Craig Aurness (West Light); *r,* Francolon (Gamma-Liason). **80:** *l,* Osamu Hashimoto (Sygma); *r,* Mermet/Figaro (Gamma-Liason). **82–83:** © 1939 Lowe's Incorprated Ren. 1966 Metro-Goldwyn-Mayer Inc. (Museum of Modern Art/Film Stills Archive). **86–87:** © 1939 Lowe's Incorporated Ren. 1966 Metro-Goldwyn-Mayer Inc. (Bettmann Archive). **88:** Smithsonian Institution Photo No. 81-5294A. **102–103:** George B. Schaller. **104:** *tl,* George B. Schaller; *r,* Art Wolfe. **105:** *l,* Art Wolfe; *r,* George B. Schaller. **106:** Marty Stouffer Prod. (Animals Animals). **107:** *t, b,* Xinhua News Agency (Picture Group). **108:** *r,* Art Wolfe. **109:** Joan L. Cohen (Photo Researchers). **110:** George B. Schaller. **112:** UPI/Bettmann Newsphotos. **122:** © 1937–1938, Chicago Tribune Company, all rights reserved, used with permission. **126–135:** Ken O'Donoghue © D.C. Heath. **140:** Courtesy of Clyde Robert Bulla. **276:** Courtesy of Bradbury Press.
Photo Coordinator: Connie Komack. **Photo Research:** Martha Friedman. **Photo Styling:** Nanci Lindholm.